Changing Classics in Schools

Bob Lister

CAMBRIDGE
UNIVERSITY PRESS

To Sue and Ian

CAMBRIDGE UNIVERSITY PRESS
Cambridge, New York, Melbourne, Madrid, Cape Town, Singapore, São Paulo

Cambridge University Press
The Edinburgh Building, Cambridge CB2 8RU, UK

www.cambridge.org
Information on this title: www.cambridge.org/9780521677745

First published 2007

Printed in the United Kingdom at the University Press, Cambridge

A catalogue record for this publication is available from the British Library

ISBN 978-0-521-67774-5 paperback

Contents

Foreword

In many respects classics is in better health than it has been for thirty years. In the world of the arts and media, ancient Greece and Rome continue to intrigue, entertain, influence and motivate. TV viewers are eagerly awaiting the second series of the HBO/BBC/RAI co-production *Rome*, which will chart the course of the civil conflict that followed the assassination of Julius Caesar. Two years ago film buffs had Wolfgang Petersen's *Troy* and Oliver Stone's *Alexander*, and are about to get *300*, the film of Frank Miller's graphic novel on Thermopylae, with perhaps a second Thermopylae film not too far off. Robert Harris has followed his success with *Pompeii* by embarking on a three-book series set in first-century BC Rome, of which the first, *Imperium*, was published to good reviews last year. Grayson Perry has revived the use of ceramic vessels as the fields for figurative scenes and several of his pieces also refer to the shapes of Greek pottery. The last eighteen months have averaged a new production of a Greek play every month in Britain, Ireland and the USA alone. It is especially interesting that in theatre there seems to be a trend towards the appropriation of Greek theatre by non-European, especially African, playwrights and directors, demonstrating that classical forms and content are 'good to think with' across cultural traditions.

In educational institutions too, classics is far from being at death's door. Every year around 600,000 children move from primary to secondary school in England with some formal study of ancient Greece and Rome under their belts, and have been doing so now for over ten years; that is just about every child currently in a maintained school in England and more: one and a half school generations. The number of entrants for Classical Civilisation and Ancient History at A level has remained steady for several years, and while Latin and Greek combined have an entry a third of that of Classical Civilisation and Ancient History, they too have held fairly steady over the last five years. The number of students taking classical subjects as either single or joint honours at university continues a gentle annual rise that has been occurring since 2000.

It has not been often that classicists have been able to experience relief if not actual pleasure at the prospect of new proposals for the National Curriculum, but that has been the case both with the publication in 2003 of *Excellence and Enjoyment: A Strategy for Primary Schools* and with the consultation proposals for the Secondary Curriculum Review published in February 2007. Both documents advocate a more flexible approach to the curriculum, giving schools greater autonomy in selecting curricular content to match the needs of their children and in tailoring the curriculum to local priorities and opportunities. Admittedly, at primary level this could weaken the study of ancient Greece and Rome in that schools are free to give them less emphasis in the history curriculum. However, it is not likely that schools will rush on a large scale to abandon subject matter which they have planned and resourced themselves to teach and which has provided valuable learning for their children over several years. Teachers have learned that children enjoy engaging with Greek myths and that the Greeks offer excellent potential for topic work where art, citizenship, music, English and history, for example, branch from a single theme; many schools have Romano-British sites nearby, which they have built very effectively into their local studies courses. In addition, the flexibility of the strategy means that some schools may choose to make more of their existing classical components and that there are opportunities to provide experience of the classical world outside the more familiar subject structure.

It is at secondary level that there has been the most significant reduction in the amount of classics taught and that the pain at the decline of classics has been most acutely felt. At first glance, the Secondary Curriculum Review document offers little to cheer. The Roman Empire, which featured as compulsory in the original programme of study for History and was made optional in the Dearing Review of 1993, has now completely disappeared. There is now no direct reference to pupils studying anything prior to the early medieval period. However, anyone thinking for a moment that the current Secondary Curriculum Review would specify subject matter at that level of detail is out of touch with the direction taken by educational policy over the last five years. Naturally, the Secretary of State is going to bow to some cultural pressures in defiance of the Qualifications and Curriculum Authority (QCA) and require study of certain authors in English and of the British Empire in History, but this is not likely to be extensive and will not include classics. It is the overall tenor of the Review that is important, as its principal focus is to define the curriculum in terms of children's needs. In doing so, QCA emphasises the personal development of the child, the qualities and skills young people need to succeed in school and in adult life. There is a stress on personalising the curriculum and an endorsement of flexible curriculum and classroom provision in order to provide young people with experiences appropriate to their learning needs and interests. It is these that subjects are seen to serve, and when assessing the role of a subject in the curriculum, headteachers and curriculum planners will need to look for its capacity to produce particular learning outcomes. The good news for classics teachers is that the outcomes are content free – they are broad skills and dispositions rather than propositional knowledge and specific skills. Therefore, if classics is to have a role to play in the secondary curriculum, it needs to be able to demonstrate two things: first, its impact – that it delivers certain learning outcomes for the young people who study it and how these outcomes relate to those of other subjects; second, the feasibility of including it in the curriculum – that there are resources to support it in terms of access to suitably qualified teachers, to learning materials and to time and opportunity.

Bob Lister's book is timely in that it is not fundamentally about the parlous state of classics in schools or about the history of its decline or about the cultural reasons why everyone should study Greece and Rome. Rather, Bob raises issues about the role of classics in the school curriculum by focusing on the experience of teaching and learning in classics in two curriculum research projects he has run, one in primary schools and one in secondary. Both projects were implemented by Bob when he was Director of the Cambridge School Classics Project and follow in the tradition of CSCP's emphasis on action research. His discussion of the projects triangulates among the aims, aspirations and experiences of the participants and stresses the need to see the links in learning between classics and other subjects. In basing his conclusions about learning in these projects on formal research he indicates the direction classics teachers are going to need to follow in order to meet the demands of the flexible curriculum for demonstrable impact on learners. He also addresses from a solid research base the expectations headteachers are likely to have for the feasibility of maintaining or introducing classics into the curriculum, exploring how it might be possible to provide sustained individualised experiences to meet the needs and interests of pupils in contexts where there is no existing provision of classics. Current changes to Postgraduate Certificate in Education (PGCE) courses are bringing them into a closer relationship to study at MA level. This should foster a favourable environment for PGCE trainees and their mentors in school to carry forward the research agenda and expand the evidence base for claims about learning in classics. If classics teachers follow the route Bob Lister indicates in this book, if they rise to the challenges and opportunities of the revised secondary curriculum with the determination and flexibility they have shown in the various crises of the last forty years, the future for classics in maintained schools could be brighter than it has been for some time.

Richard Woff
Head of Schools and Young Audiences Education
The British Museum

Acknowledgements

I could not have written this book without the support and dedication of the many people who worked with me on the two curriculum development projects I undertook as Director of the Cambridge School Classics Project, the Iliad Project and the Cambridge Online Latin Project.

The Iliad Project, the focus of the first half of the book, was CSCP's first primary curriculum initiative but in its emphasis on storytelling it drew heavily on Martin Forrest's pioneering work in the late 1960s and early 1970s, which led to the publication of the Greek World Foundation Course. I would particularly like to thank Grant Bage, with whom I co-directed the project, and Hugh Lupton and Daniel Morden, the creators of *War with Troy*, for the expertise and imagination they brought to the project. I would also like to acknowledge the contribution of Janet Dyson and David Reedy in Barking and Dagenham local authority and of teachers and pupils in the participating Dagenham schools (Godwin Primary School, Parsloes Primary School, St Joseph's Catholic Primary School, St Peter's Catholic Primary School, William Bellamy Junior School and William Ford Junior School), and especially Anne Fitzpatrick, Liz Lloyd and Bobbie Gargrave.

The Cambridge Online Latin Project, to which the second half of the book is devoted, grew out of a very small research and development project whose team (Vicky Berriman, Ann Dodgson, Paul Jackson, Jo Mullins, Andrew Wilson) deserve special credit for giving the project such a solid foundation. The project was also heavily dependent on the work of the Cambridge Latin Course revision team (Patricia Acres, Eileen Emmett, Jean Hubbard, Debbie James, Pat Story). The main phase of the project involved more than fifty people at its height, amongst whom I would like to thank in particular Jill Dalladay, Roger Dalladay, Robin Griffin, Will Griffiths, Martin Hodge, Joe Hunnable, Ann Hunt, Maria Kilby, Wilf O'Neill, Sue Pemberton, Panos Seranis and Tony Smith. I would also like to express my warmest thanks to Maire Collins and Sheila Skilbeck in the CSCP office for their hard work, patience and support.

I owe a great debt of gratitude to Pat Story, David Taylor and Richard Woff for their constructive criticism of early drafts of the book, which led to much stimulating discussion and, occasionally, substantial re-writing.

Finally, I would also like to thank the PGCE Classics panel (Eileen Emmett, Jonathan Green, Steve Hunt and Bar Roden) who took on my PGCE responsibilities while I was on study leave writing the book.

Abbreviations

AQA	The Assessment and Qualifications Alliance
Becta	British Educational Communications and Technology Agency
CLC	Cambridge Latin Course
COLP	The Cambridge Online Latin Project
CSCP	The Cambridge School Classics Project
DES	The Department of Education and Science (created 1964)
DfEE	The Department for Education and Employment (created 1995)
DfES	The Department for Education and Skills (created 2001)
GCSE	General Certificate of Secondary Education
GRIPS	Greeks and Romans in Primary Schools
HMI	Her Majesty's Inspector(ate)
ICT	information and communication technology
JACT	The Joint Association of Classical Teachers
LA	local authority (formerly LEA, local education authority)
LACT	London Association of Classical Teachers
NLS	The National Literacy Strategy
Ofsted	The Office for Standards in Education
PGCE	Postgraduate Certificate in Education
QCA	Qualifications and Curriculum Authority
SAT	Standard Assessment Task
VC	video conference

Introduction

1 | Civilisation and language

The decision by Oxford and Cambridge in 1960 to remove Latin as an entry requirement marked the beginning of a very unsettled period in classics teaching, involving both much-needed reform instigated by classicists themselves and unwelcome changes forced on classicists by external agencies unaware of, or indifferent to, the precarious state of the subject in schools. A range of indicators emphasises the extent to which classics has been marginalised in schools since that time. In the early 1970s there were eight inspectors for classics in Her Majesty's Inspectorate (HMI), now there are none; in 1972 there were twenty-one University Departments of Education offering a postgraduate certificate in education (PGCE),[1] now there are three – Cambridge, King's College London and Strathclyde – although the course at Strathclyde has not run in two of the last three years; in 1986 there were thirty-five approved syllabuses in classical subjects (eight Latin, five Greek, fifteen classical civilisation and seven combined language and civilisation courses) for the newly introduced General Certificate of Secondary Education (GCSE) examinations (Baldock 1986: 5), but from autumn 2006 this was reduced to four (one Latin, one Greek and two classical civilisation); in 1974 nearly half of all comprehensive schools offered some form of classics (DES 1977: 17), but by 1988 the figure had dropped to between a third and a quarter (DES 1988: 39), and by 2005 it had dropped again to fewer than one in ten (for a detailed analysis of current provision see chapter 7); membership of the Joint Association of Classical Teachers (JACT) dropped from 1,900 in 1988 to just over 1,000 in 2006; since 2000 there have been fewer than a hundred candidates a year for A level Latin from non-selective maintained schools (from a total of more than 2,500 schools).

These are sobering statistics but, without the energy and imagination of the many classicists who have contributed to the re-

---

[1] See Dowden (1983), pp.16–18.

invention of classics to meet the changing needs and expectations of schools and their pupils, it is highly unlikely that there would be any classics in non-selective maintained schools today. Two curriculum developments in the late 1960s and early 1970s made it possible to 'sell' classics in comprehensive schools: classical civilisation courses for the lower secondary years, which required no knowledge of the classical languages; and story-based Latin courses. Ongoing work on these two developments forms the main focus of this book. The first part of the book considers the work of the Iliad Project, which was set up to support the teaching on the ancient Greeks at Key Stage 2 and led to the creation of a new oral retelling of the story of the Trojan War specifically for nine- to eleven-year-olds. The second part looks at the Cambridge Online Latin Project and the role of information and communication technology in supporting the learning of Latin and providing access to the subject for pupils in schools with no classics teacher. The remainder of this chapter establishes the context for these two developments: it examines the relationship between the civilisation and language strands of classics; revisits the debate, often heated, about their place in the school curriculum; and reflects on the way the teaching of classics has changed since the early 1960s.

Classical civilisation and the case for classics

There has been a long tradition of emphasising the cultural legacy of the ancient world in putting forward the case for classics.[2] Cultural aspects of classics have been used to justify the place of classics in the curriculum even by those who, in the classroom, placed the emphasis firmly on the teaching of the languages. So, for instance, the 1961 edition of *The Teaching of Classics*, which represented the views of the Incorporated Association of Assistant Masters in Secondary Education, argued that we can learn from the 'experiments' of the Greek and Roman world:

> Relative to the modern world their activities were limited and their achievements on a tiny scale. This very characteristic makes them more easy of comprehension. Their records are brief and their ways almost endearingly simple. As we examine the

---

[2] See for instance the 1921 government report, *The Classics in Education*, which opens with an unequivocal statement: 'The civilisation of the modern western world is grounded upon the ancient civilisation of the Mediterranean coast ... A very large part of our present civilisation cannot be understood without some knowledge of its predecessor. Our ideas of law, citizenship, freedom and empire; our poetry and prose literature; our political, metaphysical, aesthetic, and moral philosophy, indeed our organised rational pursuit of truth in all its non-experimental branches, as well as a large and vital part of the religion which had won to itself so much of the civilised world, are rooted in the art or thought of that ancient civilisation' (London, HMSO, p. 6).

picture we find that the foreground is not cluttered with distracting detail. Classical literature is indeed reputed for its objectivity, which is only matched by the objectivity with which the dispassionate reader may now study the story. Our own mental camera is not obscured by the kind of emotional prejudices which can fog the picture when we study our national history or present-day affairs.

> ... One may remain innocent of the declensions and still admire the massive and efficient grandeur of a Roman aqueduct, without knowing the Greek alphabet one may be charmed by the balanced grace of a Greek temple or enthralled by the exquisite but unaffected perfection of an Attic red-figure vase.
>
> (IAAMSS 1961: 2–3)

But the authors make it clear that appreciation of cultural heritage must go hand in hand with knowledge of the classical languages:

> Yet strangely enough this contention is true only up to a point. The Greekless and Latinless soon begin to be aware, however dim their apprehension, that something is missing.
>
> (IAAMSS 1961: 3)

In fact, real appreciation of classical art and architecture, it is argued, is 'to some extent dependent on a knowledge of Greek and Latin' and 'the same, but without any qualification, is *a fortiori* true of classical literature' (p. 3). Literature in translation is rejected out of hand because the excellence of classical literature 'lies not in the story so much as the manner of its telling' (p. 4); and, in support of the study of the classical languages, it is argued further that such study provides much-needed mental training:

> A study that calls for a close inspection of the written word, for careful scrutiny instead of 'the once-over' – that characteristic coinage of recent times – for disciplined thinking in place of slip-shod guesswork, is a study that has its part to play in keeping the jungle back from civilization. The skills that Latin demands are sorely needed in a world where loose thought and careless speech are rife.
>
> (IAAMSS 1961: 5)

The introduction closes with a reminder that classics 'represents some episodes in man's history when he was at his best, when the individual counted for most, when, in spite of limited resources he achieved the most' (p. 6), and a plea that all, not just the favoured few, should be given access to the subject. Aware, no doubt, of the elitist tag attached to Latin and Greek, the authors of *The Teaching of Classics* subsumed the dubious case for classics as a mental training within the more inclusive cultural argument. But the rhetoric in no way matched the reality: in most classrooms classics meant Latin and Greek, with the emphasis firmly on 'the acquisition of linguistic skills of translation (in both directions) in their written form' (Forrest 1996: 2), with little or no time spent on aqueducts, temples or red-figure vases.

However, the decision by Oxford and Cambridge, reached separately within a few months in 1960, to remove Latin as a matriculation requirement had already forced the classics community to examine in the closest detail the case for classics and tensions between the arguments for its inclusion in the curriculum and the practical realities of classroom teaching. A key forum for discussion was a series of conferences organised by JACT and the JACT journal, *Didaskalos*. The general tone of the debate was set by the first article in the first issue, R. R. Bolgar's article entitled 'A theory of classical education'[3] in which he spelt out his concerns about placing undue emphasis on the linguistic case for classics:

> When we try to justify a Latin course which has the learning of the language for its aim without reference to the study of literature, the arguments that lie to hand are unconvincing. They are unlikely to lead our contemporaries to change their minds about the merits of the classical discipline. The advantages offered by the language as such are too slight and too nebulous to provide reasonable grounds for the expenditure of so much educational time and effort. If we want a persuasive argument to support Latin studies we shall have to look elsewhere than to the interest of grammar and the training provided by the practice of translation.
>
> (Bolgar 1963: 16)

It went on to re-state the case for teaching classics for its cultural legacy:

> The future of classical learning depends on our being able to show that it makes a valid contribution to man's understanding of his world and therefore to the betterment of life. We must therefore, in considering the possibilities of the subject, take our stand on the fund of human experience which it reveals to us. The educational possibilities of the classical heritage are manifestly great.
>
> (Bolgar 1963: 17)

Bolgar wanted to see classicists focus on 'the study of ancient institutions, customs and ways of thought' (p. 20), linked closely to the study of classical literature. Aware that what he was proposing might

---

[3] This was the first in a series of six articles examining the classical education from a range of perspectives.

be seen as revolutionary and a move into the territory of anthropologists and sociologists, he argued that such a focus would in fact require nothing more than a shift in emphasis, a shift he saw as 'beginning already as a feature of the natural development of the subject' (p. 21). In particular he wanted a re-orientation in the approach to literature both in universities and in schools. This would necessitate a change in the approach to the teaching of Latin in schools:

> Reorganised with the primary aim of promoting reading knowledge, even a short Latin course should allow for the study of several books with ample time for comment ... In the final analysis, the whole burden will fall on the shoulders of the teaching profession. If they can develop an approach to their material which chimes in with contemporary interests, classical studies will flourish. If they cannot do this, Latin's day is done.
>
> (Bolgar 1963: 25)

This line of argument found little favour with traditionalists such as T. W. Melluish, who had been a driving force behind *The Teaching of Classics*. Melluish, as Martin Forrest notes (Forrest 1996: 62), was one of the few people willing to say publicly what undoubtedly many other classicists believed privately, that the tone of *Didaskalos* was unnecessarily and unhelpfully pessimistic about the future of classics and that any attempts to water down the emphasis on language (by which he meant attempts to remove prose composition) would rapidly lead to the demise of Latin. As Melluish himself put it:

> Experimental linguistic 'appreciation' papers and questions involving the 'recognition' of constructions seem a good deal less attractive than the bulk of the baby's bathwater, and if swallowed by the baby would cause its rapid decline.
>
> (Melluish 1966: 54)

As we know, Melluish lost the battle. Although prose composition was not abolished, it became optional. New ways of testing language were introduced, and literary appreciation was incorporated into set text examinations at the expense of questions on grammar. Other developments marked a serious attempt by classicists to ensure that classics in schools put the cultural heritage of the ancient world centre stage: Moses Finley masterminded the creation of JACT Ancient History as an academically demanding source-based A level course; classical civilisation courses, from foundation level (Key Stage 3) through to A level, were introduced; and story-based language courses were developed (the Cambridge Latin Course in England, Ecce Romani in Scotland) with the twin aims of teaching comprehension of

Latin through reading and of fostering an understanding of the cultural context of Roman civilisation. But these developments did not bring about the Dark Ages envisaged by T. W. Melluish, who imagined a morning one day when the minister would take his watch from his pocket and say, 'At this precise moment no single boy in the United Kingdom is doing a Latin Prose' (Melluish 1966: 50). While one section of the classics community, particularly but by no means exclusively those teaching in comprehensive schools, embraced 'new' classics, another, at the other end of the spectrum, strove successfully to maintain as much of the traditional curriculum as possible. The result is that prose composition continues to be taught in some schools today and remains an option in classical Greek and Latin A level.

Traditional classics in action

I myself am a product of a hardline form of traditional classics: the same month that Melluish was writing about the fast approaching Dark Ages, I, having already studied Latin for five years and Greek for two, was sitting the scholarship papers for Shrewsbury School.[4] Of the papers I sat, the most memorable (because it was the most difficult) was the Latin Verse composition paper, the last three questions on which were as follows:

3. Translate into Latin Elegiacs:

    May-you-leave my window, (whether being) a-slow-woman or with-faster foot.

    What (is it) to-me, so-long-as you-leave? You-seek help badly from-hence.

    Seek a-strong man: that-man will-shelter you well being-afraid.

    That-man will-shelter, whether you-may-have-behaved yourself well or badly.

    That-man will-give what you-desire. However he-is to-be-sought from-elsewhere;

    Such a-burden never will-be-undertaken by-me (Dative).

    Run-away. It-was time. Hasten your-steps with-silent foot.

    I am not (a man) whom a-woman may-be-able to-trust.

---

[4] Shrewsbury School was, of course, a bastion of traditional classics. Forrest notes that 'the basis of the traditional classical education to be found in the mid- twentieth-century English public and grammar schools may ... be recognised a hundred years previously at Shrewsbury' (Forrest 1996: 2).

4. Write a Latin poem, however short, to do with the World Cup.

5. Translate, as freely as you like, into Latin Verse:

> Of all the things that can be done
> to pass a summer's afternoon
> I cannot think of any worse
> than writing Elegiac verse.

The examination rubric may have been friendly ('Do as many, or as few, questions as you like, in any order you like') but was hardly reassuring for the thirteen-year-olds facing these fiendishly difficult questions. The paper was, I have always assumed, the work of Mark Mortimer, a brilliant classical scholar and the 'narrow-minded linguist' of the *Didaskalos* article of the same name, which took the form of an exchange of letters with John Roberts, at the time head of classics at Eton College, in which Mortimer put up a determined defence of the classical languages as the unique selling point of the classical education:

> if Classics has a particular *educational* value, not shared by Modern History, say, or Eng. Lit., it will lie not in people, politics or pots, but in the study of, juxtaposed with our own, the Greek and Latin *languages*, their development, morphology and syntax, and, more to the point, since Philology has never in fact been taken seriously as an educational subject, in the exercise of *translation*, of decoding messages in one language and re-encoding them in another, structurally different, one. From this point of view the end-product of the Classical Education is simply an ability to say what one means and understand what one hears – not, perhaps, as may have been claimed, a *sine qua non* of Leadership and the Art of Government, but still an indispensable preliminary to most human pursuits. And to *this* end any study, however diverting, of the *subject matter* and *background* of Classical Literature, and of the Classical World in general, contributes nothing except as sugar on the intellectual pill, rendering it more palatable to the majority of students whose interests are not, or not exclusively, linguistic.
>
> (Roberts and Mortimer 1967: 101)

No genuflection here in the direction of cultural heritage. And Mortimer's teaching was in line with his principles: when reading, say, the *Metamorphoses* or the *Aeneid*, discussion of historical context, let alone authorial purpose, was not merely discouraged but positively forbidden; the business of literature lessons was translation. Translation was, of course, supplemented by prose composition. This narrowly linguistic approach, as advocated and practised by Mortimer and Melluish, worked at a particular time in the hands of particular teachers in schools of a particular type; although, as Mark Mortimer himself acknowledged, even in schools like Shrewsbury the interests of most students were not linguistic and already by the end of the 1960s Oxford and Cambridge's decision to remove Latin as a matriculation requirement was having a noticeable impact and schools such as Shrewsbury were seeing a significant drop in the numbers choosing Latin for O level.

'New' classics in action

What worked in independent schools and grammar schools in the 1960s – and continues to work in just a few schools today – would not have worked in a comprehensive school in the 1970s. John Sharwood Smith's description of an imaginary day in the life of a fictitious classics teacher in a comprehensive school (though 'not quite imaginary and not quite fictitious, as the lessons are a conflation of many lessons I have seen and the teacher an amalgam of some four teachers I know well' (Sharwood Smith 1977: 76)) painted a very different picture. His day begins with a Year 8 Latin lesson on an early stage of the Cambridge Latin Course,[5] followed by an ancient history lesson (with *three* sixth formers!) looking at the Culture of Athens option from the JACT ancient history A level syllabus; after break he teaches a double lesson on Theseus and the Minotaur with a mixed ability classical studies group in the school hall; lunch is taken up with a voluntary Greek class; and in the afternoon, he has a CSE[6] class working on projects for ancient technology, followed by a Latin O level class studying *Aeneid* IV:

> our teacher engages the class in a discussion of Dido's behaviour on learning that she is about to be deserted by Aeneas. Why is she described as raging like a Bacchanal through the streets of her city? Is this, perhaps, to cool the lively sympathy we feel for her; and to hint at the superiority of Aeneas, whose emotions are no less passionate but more under control? Since both are leaders and responsible for the well-being of their followers, ought not duty, however disagreeable, to come before passion?
>
> There is no difficulty in persuading the girls to talk. The girls, who are in a majority, are quick to nail Aeneas as a Male Chauvinist Pig, and our teacher has a hard time preventing Virgil's complex and ambivalent treatment of Dido from being grossly oversimplified.
>
> (Sharwood Smith 1977: 79)

---

[5] Year 8 refers to pupils aged twelve at the start of the academic year. See appendix 3 for further information on National Curriculum terminology.
[6] The Certificate of Secondary Education was the lower tier, and O level the higher tier, of public examinations at sixteen before the introduction of the General Certificate of Secondary Education in 1986.

The contrast with my own school experience of literature lessons could not be greater. But of course it was not only teachers in the growing number of comprehensive schools who had moved away from the narrowly linguistic approach to Latin and were devoting time to the discussion and appreciation of literature. As we saw earlier, Mark Mortimer's adversary in *Didaskalos* was the head of classics at Eton College; another champion of literary criticism was Maurice Balme, the head of classics at Harrow School, whose *Aestimanda*, regarded by many as a landmark in the teaching of literary criticism in schools, upset Mortimer because he felt unable to answer the questions (Roberts and Mortimer 1967: 112–13)! Balme had already written in the first issue of *Didaskalos* that 'in the sixth form the main emphasis [when teaching literature] must be ... on the matter; the study of the language must be seen only as a means to understanding the thought' (Balme 1963: 102) and concluded by saying that 'the traditional curriculum is clearly due for revision, which will cut out all that hinders the enjoyment of the classics as a living literature and which will help to make their relevance clear' (p. 106).

Classics for all or classics for the few?

Nevertheless, there were divisions between independent and some grammar schools on the one hand and comprehensive schools on the other, brought into sharp focus in Stephen Sharp's often-quoted *Didaskalos* article.

> We continue to squander manpower in small sixth-form teaching groups, and accept a reputation for mild eccentricity as the price we pay for not having to teach more than the most able pupils. The storm has been weathered, and out of it have come vastly improved courses for the academic élite. JACT Ancient History and Cambridge Latin represent a considerable advance, but they are only marginally relevant to the school where I teach. The widespread reorganization of the nineteen-sixties gave us classicists a fine opportunity to contribute to education more widely: in many cases we simply constructed impregnable defences on undisputed territory. At meetings of Classics teachers up and down the country these past three years, an urgent desire to use Classics in the education of children has been less in evidence than that peculiar freemasonry based on sherry, Oxbridge colleges and textual criticism.
>
> (Sharp 1973: 276)

While reformers in the 1960s might have been united in their commitment to changing the content and teaching of the classics curriculum, their apparent solidarity, according to Sharp, hindered frank discussion of the part classics should play in schools. He felt that discussion was dominated by questions concerning the effective transmission of the achievement of Greece and Rome rather than the educational needs of pupils, *all* pupils, and the ways in which teachers, 'who happen to have a classical training', could help meet those needs: in the words of John Sharwood Smith (1977: 9), Sharp was primarily interested in education *through* classics rather than education *in* classics.[7] To what extent were classicists willing and able to make classics accessible and inclusive? This question was raised in a report on a conference organised by Sharwood Smith on 'Classical Studies in Education Today' and the author had no doubt as to classicists' responsibilities:

> In case there is any sneaking arrière pensée that an interest in Classical Studies without the Languages represents only an undignified effort to safeguard tomorrow's bread and butter, let it be said firmly that it is a very different matter – it is a question of the frank courageous acceptance by Classical teachers of their share in the responsibility for the education of the great mass of our children who are academically less able: we never did have the right to opt out of it, to confine our efforts to the 'cream', and the fact that we have been allowed to do so has been not only unjust to others but unhealthy for ourselves.
>
> (*Latin Teaching* XXXII(2), June 1966: 55)

By the mid-1970s classical studies courses had been introduced in many schools, but there were still concerns about the way the subject was viewed by classicists themselves. Sharwood Smith thought there was a danger that some classicists saw the function of classical studies as keeping the classics teacher in employment 'so that he can continue his proper task, which is the teaching of Latin and Greek to a select few', and using it as 'a bait to catch bright pupils for next year's Latin beginners' class' (Sharwood Smith 1977: 8). Underlying this view was the sense that classical studies was the poor relation of the classics world. In spite of Sharwood Smith's concerns, classical studies (or classical civilisation as it became more commonly known) became increasingly popular at public examination level, particularly A level. But even after the introduction of the National Curriculum in 1988, and the inclusion of two classical civilisation topics in the history curriculum for primary schools, Bob Young felt it necessary to write:

> If we are serious about 'classics for all' we need to begin with

---

[7] The work of Stephen Sharp and Steve Woodward, his colleague at Dinnington High School, is discussed in chapter 3.

what it should be offering to everyone, then consider how this can be enriched and extended for some – not the other way round. This means ending arid arguments which set classical civilisation and the classical language in competition; blurring (not eliminating) the boundaries between 'language' and 'non-linguistic' courses; and disposing once and for all of the dangerous snobbery that sees the function of classics (usually, in practice, Latin) as being to 'sort out the sheep from the goats'.

(Young 1991: 3)

As Martin Forrest comments, the arrival of the National Curriculum was 'something of a bitter-sweet experience' (Forrest 1996: 150): while it provided an entitlement to classical civilisation at primary level, it reduced opportunities to study classical languages at secondary level. But in spite of Chris Stray's statement that the lack of reference to classics in the National Curriculum shows 'just how marginalised a subject has become which once lay at the heart of English high culture' (Stray 1998: 1), more children in England are required to study classics (albeit in the form of classical civilisation) than at any time previously. The fact that all children in England must study ancient Greece and the Romans in Britain as part of their compulsory education means that classicists *must* take 'classics for all' seriously. That is the starting point for this book. Part I considers how classicists can best exploit the opportunities for offering classics for all at the upper end of primary school, and Part II examines how new technologies can help make Latin available and accessible to a wide range of pupils in secondary schools.

References

Baldock, M. (1986). *GCSE* (JACT pamphlet). London: JACT

Balme, M. (1963). 'Sixth form studies: classical literature – 1', *Didaskalos* 1(1), pp. 101–6

Bolgar, R. R. (1963). 'A theory of classical education', *Didaskalos* 1(1), pp. 5–26

DES (1977). *Classics in Comprehensive Schools*. London: HMSO

DES (1988). *Classics from 5 to 16, Curriculum Matters 12*. London: HMSO

Dowden, K. (1983). 'But who will teach the teachers?', *Latin Teaching* XXXVI(3), pp.16–18

Forrest, M. (1996). *Modernising the Classics: A Study in Curriculum Development*. Exeter: Exeter University Press

IAAMSS (Incorporated Association of Assistant Masters in Secondary Schools) (1961). *The Teaching of Classics*. Cambridge: Cambridge University Press

Melluish, T. W. (1966). 'Latin prose composition', *Latin Teaching* XXXII(2), pp. 50–4

Roberts, J. and Mortimer, M. (1967). 'The narrow-minded linguist', *Didaskalos* 2(2), pp. 100–14

Sharp, S. (1973). 'Classical studies – the medium not the message', *Didaskalos* 4(2), pp. 276–89

Sharwood Smith, J. E. (1977). *On Teaching Classics*. London: Routledge and Kegan Paul

Stray, C. (1998). *Classics Transformed: Schools, Universities and Society in England, 1830–1960*. Oxford: Clarendon Press

Young, B. (1991). 'The new face of classics', *JACT Review* 2(10), pp. 2–4

2 | Classics and the primary curriculum

For all the problems that the National Curriculum has caused for classics at secondary level, classicists nevertheless have reason to be grateful for its introduction in so far as it established an entitlement for all pupils in England and Wales (though since devolution this now applies only to England) to learn about classical history and culture within the compulsory curriculum as part of Key Stage 2 history. This chapter looks at the benefits and drawbacks of locating classics within history, and then examines the possibilities for adopting a cross-curricular approach to classics at Key Stage 2 to include elements of English and literacy (as set out in the National Literacy Strategy), as well as history.

Before 1988, it was largely the expertise and interests of individual teachers that determined whether or not children learnt about the classical world at primary school level: while some primary school teachers read Greek myths and legends with their classes and taught aspects of classical history such as Roman Britain and the Olympic Games, many children left primary school having had little or no contact with the classical world. It is not surprising, therefore, that classicists assumed that within the state school system classics education began at secondary school. Even John Sharwood Smith, who had a better understanding than anyone of the place of classics in the wider educational context, makes no mention of classics in the primary curriculum in *On Teaching Classics*, published in 1977. But within ten years HMI's *Curriculum Matters* series, designed to stimulate discussion about the 5 to 16 curriculum in the lead-up to the introduction of the National Curriculum, put classics at primary level firmly on the agenda: almost a quarter of *Classics from 5 to 16 (Curriculum Matters 12)* was devoted to the teaching of classical civilisation in the primary and early secondary years (DES 1988: 5–14).

Starting from the premise that to be included in the National Curriculum classics had to offer something for all pupils, HMI argued that there were two main reasons for studying the classical world: 'its intrinsic interest, and its capacity to increase pupils' understanding of themselves and of the world in which they live' (DES 1988: 2). This emphasis on pupils' personal and social education reflected the changes in approaches to classics teaching set in motion in the 1960s, in particular the growth of classical civilisation courses, and paved the way for classics to be included under humanities rather than languages in the National Curriculum. HMI envisaged a National Curriculum on broad areas of experience as outlined in *Curriculum Matters 2* (DES 1985), and set out the contribution classics could make within and across these areas (including the mathematical, scientific and technical). The National Curriculum as implemented, however, provided less flexibility, because it was subject-based, and classics was confined to three compulsory study units in history, two at Key Stage 2 (Ancient Greece and Roman Britain – though the latter was only part of a study unit on invaders) and one at Key Stage 3 (the Roman Empire).

With the removal of the Roman Empire as a core unit of Key Stage 3 history after Sir Ron Dearing's review of the National Curriculum in 1995, the presence of the classical study units in Key Stage 2 history took on even greater significance, as Richard Woff noted:

> The effect of this was to transfer the principal onus for public education about the Greek and Roman worlds from secondary to primary schools. The continuing presence of Greece and Roman Britain in the Key Stage 2 programmes of study means that all children in state education, and probably the majority in private schools, engage in some study of both the classical cultures before the age of 11. For all but the tiniest minority of these children, that it is the sum total of their experience of the classical world in formal education.
>
> (Woff 2003: 172)

Given that the experience of classics for more than nine in ten children was limited to what they encountered at primary school, one might have expected classicists to have devoted a significant amount of time, effort and money into resources to support hard-pressed primary school teachers trying to implement the compulsory study units on ancient Greece and the Romans in Britain with, in most cases, very little subject knowledge. But in fact, as Woff says, 'the success of establishing classics firmly in the primary curriculum was followed up with surprisingly little practical support in the world of classics education' other than two projects undertaken by Martin Forrest, who was a lecturer in primary education in Bristol, in conjunction with two local primary school teachers,[1] and a series of six booklets produced by JACT.[2]

This lack of action on the part of classicists was, however, understandable. Secondary school classics teachers were fully occupied fighting a rearguard action to save classics from further cuts to their already limited timetable allocation, particularly at Key Stage 3, and in many cases their own posts were under threat. In Derbyshire, for instance, reorganisation of educational services between 1987 and 1990 led to a reduction in the number of schools offering classical subjects from twelve to two.[3] Another reason for inaction was the lack of effective channels of communication between secondary and primary schools, at both local and national level. As a result there was little way of knowing what sort of help primary schools teachers might need, and there was a danger that any help offered might have seemed patronising.

The GRIPS report

This was the context in which the Cambridge School Classics Project set up the GRIPS (Greeks and Romans in Primary Schools) [4] project in 1997 to review the approach of teachers, parents and pupils to the classical study units of Key Stage 2 history.[5] It also coincided with the start of the review and consultation process that led to the introduction of the revised National Curriculum in 2000.

The research was based on a relatively small sample of ten schools, but the diversity of the schools' urban/rural contexts, geographical locations and catchment areas ensured a broad spread of social and cultural backgrounds, and an advantage of working with a small sample was the opportunity it provided for an in-depth examination of key issues. Over a six-month period the research team investigated the attitudes and approaches of twenty-eight teachers (of whom one had classical civilisation A level and one a degree in classics and archaeology) through lesson observation, questionnaires and follow-up interviews; conducted a survey of parental attitudes (with 227 returns from 635 questionnaires distributed); and individually interviewed 120 children,[6] whose written work in history was also recorded.

[1] For descriptions of the projects see Farrell and Forrest (1989) and Cowen (1992).
[2] The series was called *Themes: The Use of the Classical World in the National Curriculum for Primary Schools*.
[3] Unpublished paper given by David Singleton HMI in 1993 at a conference in Cambridge on the future of classics.
[4] For the full report see Bage, Grisdale and Lister (1999).
[5] See *The National Curriculum for England: History* (DfEE/QCA 1999b) for full details of the classical units.
[6] To provide as representative a sample as possible, for each of the twenty classes involved one pair of pupils, one boy and one girl, was selected by the form teacher from three broad attainment bands: below average, average and above average.

The key points to emerge from the research were that

- teachers wanted the classical units to be retained after 2000;
- teachers valued the context provided by the classical units for supporting the language and study skills of all pupils;
- parents thought that the classical units were worthwhile and relevant for their children;
- children enjoyed and were strongly motivated by the classical units.

There was very strong support from teachers for the inclusion of classical history in the primary curriculum: twenty-six of the twenty-eight teachers, when asked if they would continue teaching about ancient Greece and the Romans in Britain if they were no longer compulsory, said that they would. They felt that the classical study units created very good opportunities for pupils to extend their reading (of both fiction and non-fiction) and writing skills, and also to improve speaking skills through drama and role play. But what they valued above all was the capacity of the classical units to engage and motivate their pupils:

> There is such a wide range of work you can do ... Whatever the child's interest, there is something to catch them.
>
> (Bristol teacher)

> They really went down the paths of enquiry, to the extent that they had gone home and drawn Greek pots, gone to the library to find out information [and] written about the Greeks at home.
>
> (Bristol teacher)

> I have found these units easily capture children's imagination and interest, sparking enthusiasm for learning. They have the same effect on parents, improving home–school links and encouraging provision of educational visits and opportunities out of school.
>
> (Norfolk teacher)

Significantly, teachers also felt that the classical study units provided learning opportunities for a wide range of children, including those with special educational needs. One comment from a teacher was particularly striking:

> One special needs child has been so motivated by the myths that he has begun to read willingly and without pressure and also is now attempting to write his own 'myths'. His parents cannot believe the change in his attitude now towards work. In their words 'He has come to life'.
>
> (London teacher)

Evidence from the classroom supported this view, as can be seen from the brief extract below from observation notes on a Year 4 class of thirty-two pupils examining artefacts from ancient Greece. The observation was focused on a pupil identified as being of below average attainment in history:

> After opening discussion, a collection of artefacts and accompanying prompt sheet led to the following: 'X offers his answers to the group discussion, which are relevant and informative ... X has done extra work on the ancient Greeks and the teacher makes a real fuss of him ... he describes what he has done to the rest of the class.' Some 15 minutes later 'X is still struggling with his written work, but his motivation is so high that he keeps going.'

The observer also noted the engagement of other pupils:

> I was approached by two pupils at the end of the lesson, one to show me the ancient Greek information they had taken off the CD-ROM Encarta; the other to show me the artefact she had brought in for the teacher to use.

Such spontaneous and unprompted demonstrations of interest in the subject matter were evident in all the schools. Responses to the pupil questionnaire provided further evidence of the extent to which the classical units motivated children. When asked whether they ever chose to do work on their own on the ancient Greeks and Romans, 83 out of 120 pupils answered 'yes', evenly distributed by gender (42 boys, 41 girls) and by attainment (28 higher attaining, 28 average and 27 lower). Most of this independent work involved creative activities and what might loosely be termed 'research'. The single most common activity was reading, followed by writing and drawing. Writing activities took many forms, including building up an information file on the Romans, taking notes from library books and jotting down ideas. In several cases it was clear that pupils spent a great deal of time on their independent study:

> [I do] my own research for the topic book using library books. If I have spare time, I write about videos.
> (Year 6 girl, Gloucestershire)

> [I] take my drafting book home, stay in at play to finish off work and find out more, take my school library books home and use topic box books at school.
> (Year 6 boy, Kirklees)

The fact that two-thirds of the pupils surveyed for the GRIPS research carried on with their studies outside the classroom in this way is eloquent testimony of the subject's intrinsic interest which HMI cites as one of the main reasons for studying the classical world (DES 1988: 2). This sort of self-motivation lies at the heart of successful learning, and is particularly important to foster in subjects that are not part of the compulsory curriculum.

As well as investigating the views of teachers and pupils, the GRIPS report examined the attitudes of parents towards history generally and the Key Stage 2 classical study units in particular. Parents broadly supported the inclusion of history in the compulsory curriculum, with 94 per cent of respondents indicating that they felt their children benefited from studying the subject. A number of parents gave very full answers, for example:

> History helps to illustrate the way in which our present beliefs and attitudes were shaped. It helps us to understand how our past has formed our society. This can give children (a) pride in their own nation (b) a willingness to understand that other races/cultures are also products of their past – thus greater understanding/tolerance and less prejudice – the past is an essential component.
>
> (Essex parent)

> (1) I feel it makes/helps them to appreciate the advantages of life today – especially things like medicine and sanitation. (2) It engenders a sense of responsibility for future generations e.g. 'Looking after the world for them'. (3) Hopefully (!) it will help them not to make the same mistakes as others have, e.g. wars etc. if children understand events in the past.
>
> (Norfolk parent)

As well as feeling that their children benefited from learning about the past, a large majority of parents (78 per cent) considered that the ancient Greeks and Romans were *of significant relevance* to children today. They backed up their views with many of the arguments that classicists themselves put forward to justify their subject, citing, among other things, the significance of Greek mythology, the lessons learnt from Roman technology, the influence of the classical languages on English, and the development of democracy.

What emerged, then, from the GRIPS report was clear support for the inclusion of ancient Greece and Roman Britain in the Key Stage 2 curriculum. But the report also included one or two findings that raised questions about the actual teaching of the classical units. Firstly, many classroom activities lacked variety and challenge. An analysis of forty pupils' history topic or exercise books (comprising a total of 526 individual items of work) showed that 23 per cent of classroom work was limited to very undemanding activities such as colouring in pictures, doing word-searches, and gluing information sheets into books; a further 43 per cent required them only to copy text, e.g. word-processing information from a book and completing cloze exercises), while only 16 per cent demanded any form of extended 'original' writing.

Secondly, the teachers' coverage of topics within the classical units was very uneven. In the case of the ancient Greece unit, for example, only 'Myths and legends' were taught in great depth (see table 1), while 'Relations with other people' were covered only in basic outline – and informal discussion with teachers suggested that this was a generous assessment since, in spite of assurances of anonymity, teachers seemed apprehensive about admitting to any omissions of prescribed content. It is not surprising that some units were covered in the barest outline given the range of prescribed topics and the level of specialist knowledge required to teach them: 'Relations with other people', for example, included 'Persians, such as the stories of Marathon, Thermopylae and Salamis, the Greeks in Southern Italy, the campaigns of Alexander the Great, the influence of the Greeks on other civilisations, such as Egypt or Rome'. These are all substantial, complex areas of study which would require a great deal of research and preparation by the teacher before they could be taught to children in the seven to eleven age range. The alternative often adopted by hard-pressed teachers was to teach the topic at a very superficial level, relying on one of the many ancient Greece information books available, designed specifically for Key Stage 2 history, with a double-page spread on each topic.

Table 1   *Teachers' coverage of aspects of ancient Greece*

	Great depth	Some detail	Basic outline	Not covered
Athens and Sparta	2	11	8	0
Arts and architecture	2	16	3	0
Myths and legends	12	7	2	0
Relations with other peoples	0	7	13	1
Influence on modern world	2	14	5	0

Schemes of work for history

Changes made to Key Stage 2 history under the National Curriculum revision in 2000 were cosmetic: although the title of the study unit is now 'A European history study' rather than 'Ancient Greece', the scope and recommended content have been left unchanged. Likewise the unit on the Romans has remained much the same. What has changed since the GRIPS research was undertaken in 1998 is the extent to which primary school teachers make use of 'off-the-peg' schemes of work and lesson plans as the starting point for planning their teaching. The exponential growth of the internet and high-speed broadband access has led to a mushrooming of sites offering such support for teachers at all levels of education. Providers range from government agencies and individual teachers to commercial organisations and charities; and there is a corresponding variation in the quality of support they provide. An examination of a scheme of work produced by Qualifications and Curriculum Authority (QCA) and available in the Schemes of Work area of the DfES Standards Site highlights potential problems with such resources.[7]

For example, Unit 14 (of twenty) for Key Stage 1 and 2 history is 'Who were the ancient Greeks?', in which 'children find out about the way people lived in the ancient Greek empire'. The ancient Greek empire? Which ancient Greek empire? The seven sections into which the unit is divided (Where and when were the ancient Greeks? What were the similarities and differences between Athens and Sparta? What made the ancient Greek fighters so powerful? Was the battle of Marathon a great victory for the ancient Greeks? Who did the ancient Greeks worship and why? What happened at the theatre? What do the sources tell us about the importance of the Olympic Games to the ancient Greeks?) suggest that the unit should have been called 'Who were the fifth-century Greeks?' or perhaps 'Who were the ancient Athenians?' In spite of the section on Athens and Sparta, the notion that the ancient Greeks were a single homogeneous group whose civilisation had a fixed beginning and end pervades the unit. For instance, one suggested teaching activity is that teachers 'discuss with the children what ancient means and place the period of the ancient Greek Empire on the class time line'. This is not a helpful starting point for teaching Greek history.

Each section of the unit is broken down into learning objectives. For example, for section 3: 'What made the ancient Greek fighters so powerful?' the learning objective is that children should learn 'to infer information about Greek wars from illustrations and maps'; teaching activities include asking pupils to 'draw a detailed, labelled diagram of a Greek soldier showing his equipment, armour and weapons, and of a trireme (an ancient Greek warship)'; and learning outcomes include 'giv[ing] reasons why the Greeks needed a navy' and 'infer[ring] information about the Greek army and navy from

---

[7] The schemes of work for Key Stage 2 history are available at
http://www.standards.dfes.gov.uk/schemes2/history/his14/ (last accessed 2 December 2006).

their observations'. This detailed plan provides a tight framework for teaching Greek warfare but it may create a false sense of security in the teacher: it looks as though it provides everything the teacher needs but leaves unaddressed the underlying issue of subject-specific knowledge. Greek warfare can be taught effectively only if the teacher knows something of hoplites – and, indeed, of Greek society – or at least knows a reliable source of information, and has access to relevant primary sources from which the pupils can draw information on equipment or tactics. In many cases, the teacher will turn to the internet, where information is readily available but not necessarily either reliable or appropriate for Key Stage 2 pupils.

To sum up, while the GRIPS report provides evidence of strong support for history, and specifically classical history, among teachers and parents, it also raises concerns about the demands placed on primary school teachers and the type of support for teachers lacking the necessary subject knowledge. Recent reports from government agencies not only echo these concerns but raise other issues, which indicate that history provision, particularly at Key Stage 2, remains problematic. QCA and Ofsted draw attention to:

- the lack of priority given to history, so that 'in many primary and secondary schools, the subject is playing an increasingly marginal role in the wider curriculum' (QCA 2005: 5);

- poor planning, as a result of which 'the curriculum is piecemeal' and 'pupils end up with partial and fragmented knowledge' (Ofsted 2005a);

- 'indiscriminate, and at times slavish' use of QCA/DfES schemes of work (Ofsted 2005b);

- an imbalance between knowledge, skills and understanding, with emphasis on knowledge 'to the extent that history is little more than the acquisition of facts ... with little attempt to encourage pupils to select, organise and communicate their own work in history' (Ofsted 2005b);

- ineffective assessment – 'too few schools (less than a quarter) assess well pupils' progress in history against National Curriculum objectives and provide them with good feedback' (Ofsted 2005a);

- lessons 'insufficiently matched to the needs and abilities of pupils', with tasks that are 'undemanding and inappropriate' (Ofsted 2005b);

- 'a perception among teachers that they are increasingly having to justify time spent on history' (QCA 2005: 11) and that history is 'increasingly under pressure from the introduction of new subjects' (QCA 2005: 9).

The Annual Report 2004–5 by Her Majesty's Chief Inspector concludes the section of history in primary schools with discussion of the issue of teachers' expertise and the limited opportunities for professional development:

> Some of the problems highlighted in this report can be associated with the very limited opportunities for continuing professional development in history. The old local authority advisory structures have largely disappeared and there are only limited alternatives in place. In some LEAs there continues to be at least an annual primary history conference; some teachers are able to attend courses run by private organisations and successful clusters continue to function in good partnerships. But far too often, teachers are professionally isolated and, as a result, fail to see possibilities or have the confidence to have a go and try them. The problem is compounded by the very limited initial training that trainees are given in history. On an average PGCE primary course, the time devoted to history could be six hours training or even lower and if history is not being taught when they are working in schools, trainees may never get the chance to teach it before they are awarded qualified teacher status.
>
> (Ofsted 2005a)

Why is so little time on initial teacher training courses devoted to history (or, indeed, any specialist subject other than the core subjects)? The answer is due partly to the number of subjects that trainees have to cover in order to be able to teach the National Curriculum, and partly to the emphasis placed on developing trainees' competence in English and mathematics. This of course reflects the overall balance of the primary curriculum, where 40 per cent of every day is taken up with the literacy and numeracy hours. Aware that in some schools rigid adherence to the literacy and numeracy hours was adversely affecting teaching in non-core subjects, when the National Literacy Strategy (NLS) was relaunched as the Primary Literacy Strategy in 2003 the government actively encouraged more creative approaches to the primary curriculum, reminding schools that the Strategy was not statutory and that, for instance, schools were free to group subjects together for project work, provided there were strong enough links between the subjects.

In the case of history, the time set aside in primary schools shrank from approximately 10 per cent in the mid-1990s to as little as 3.5 per cent by 2006, by which time less than an hour a week was devoted to history in many schools.[8] In order to secure additional time for studying the classical history units, we need to look outside history and examine ways in which the classical units can be linked with other subjects to provide a coherent learning experience. In particular we need to exploit links between classics and English since so much time is devoted to the latter in primary schools.

Classics and English

There are clear links between classics and English in the primary curriculum. As has been noted elsewhere (e.g. Gay 2003), there are possibilities for introducing pupils to Greek and Roman mythology not just through the classical study units of Key Stage 2 history but also through Key Stage 2 English, which includes 'texts drawn from a variety of cultures and traditions' and 'myths, legends and traditional stories' in its list of required literature (DfEE/QCA 1999a: 26). Possibilities for contributing to the teaching of language have increased significantly with the introduction of the NLS. The challenge for classicists is to convert these possibilities into teaching modules that can be taught to all pupils as part of the mainstream curriculum. To be successful such modules need to take account of current recommended approaches to English teaching at Key Stage 2; and these are more easily identified not, as one might expect, in the National Curriculum for English but in the NLS *Framework for Teaching* (hereafter referred to as the *Framework*), published in 1998. Even though the National Curriculum for English sets out statutory requirements while the *Framework* provides only guidance, the latter tends to dominate teaching approaches in primary schools because it goes beyond the standing orders in providing '*day-to-day* reference for classroom teachers to ensure that they have appropriately high expectations of their pupils' (DfEE 1998: 2; emphasis added), prescribing not only *what* should be taught but *when*, and *how*, it should be taught.

Reactions to the introduction of the NLS have been mixed. There is no doubt that it has ensured much greater consistency of practice across primary schools and helped to raise standards by establishing clear benchmarks. Many teachers have welcomed the introduction of the NLS: for instance, feedback from 240 primary school teachers attending conferences organised by the National Literacy Trust in spring 2002 was very positive,[9] with teachers in particular appreciating:

---

[8] Figures given by Andrew Wrenn, history adviser for Cambridgeshire LA, on Radio 4, 'Making History', broadcast 13 June 2006.

[9] For a full report on the conferences go to http://www.literacytrust.org.uk/Database/ Primary/whatdoneforus.html (last accessed 2 December 2006).

- the clear learning objectives and structure, 'giving teachers a clear focus for what they teach and children a clear focus for learning – especially grammar';
- the built-in progression, continuity and consistency;
- the raised expectations for teachers and pupils.

For others, as we shall see, the NLS has brought about unwelcome changes in English teaching and raised fundamental concerns about how both language and literature are taught in primary schools.

Classics and English language

The *Framework* is a highly detailed document. It sets out term-by-term learning objectives at word, sentence and text level for every year from Year 1 to Year 6, each level with its own subdivisions. At word level the emphasis is on phonics, spelling and vocabulary; at sentence level on grammar and punctuation; and at text level on comprehension and composition. One example will give an indication of the level of detail in the *Framework*: for Year 1 Term 2 (i.e. for children aged five to six) there are forty-three learning objectives (eleven at word level, seven at sentence level and twenty-five at text level). At sentence level pupils should be taught:

Grammatical awareness

1 to expect reading to make sense and check if it does not;

2 to use awareness of the grammar of a sentence to decipher new or unfamiliar words, e.g. predict text from the grammar, read on, leave a gap and re-read;

3 to predict words from preceding words in sentences and investigate the sorts of words that 'fit', suggesting appropriate alternatives, i.e. that make sense.

Sentence construction and punctuation

4 to recognise full stops and capital letters when reading and understand how they affect the way a passage is read;

5 to continue demarcating sentences in writing, ending a sentence with a full stop;

6 to use the term *sentence* appropriately to identify sentences in text, i.e. those demarcated by capital letters and full stops;

7 to use capital letters for the personal pronoun 'I', for names and for the start of a sentence.

(DfEE 1998: 22)

The *Framework* also provides lists of technical vocabulary for word, sentence and text level work, and notes that 'most of these terms should also form part of pupils' developing vocabulary for talking about language' (DfEE 1998: 69). The technical vocabulary for Year 1 includes terms such as initial, vowel, question, blurb, character, diagram, fiction, illustrator, and non-chronological writing; for Year 6 (children aged ten to eleven) they include mnemonic, hypothesis, parentheses, assonance, kenning, obituary, synopsis and tanka.

In addition to defining the content of all literacy teaching, the *Framework* introduced the literacy hour and specified how that hour should be spent. At Key Stage 2, it recommends (DfEE 1998: 9) that teachers spend fifteen minutes on shared text work (a balance of reading and writing) with the whole class; fifteen minutes on either focused word or sentence work, again with the whole class; twenty minutes on independent reading, writing or word and sentence work, while the teacher works with at least one ability group each day on guided text work; and a final ten minutes with the whole class reviewing, reflecting, consolidating teaching points and presenting work covered in the lesson.

The *Framework* was a landmark publication not only because it demonstrated the extent to which central government was willing to dictate classroom practice, but also because, along with the publication of the follow-up resource, *Grammar for Writing* (DfEE 2000), it heralded the rehabilitation of grammar as a central element of English teaching. As the *Times Educational Supplement* said, 'it is now "all right" to teach grammar. The National Literacy Strategy and the forthcoming KS3 Strategy practically demand a more explicit treatment of knowledge about language, structure and rules.'[10] Dominic Wyse put it in stronger terms:

> The publication of the [*Framework*] and the *Grammar for Writing* resource represented the strongest emphasis on the teaching of grammar in England since the turn of the twentieth century.
>
> (Wyse 2006: 32)

Classicists frequently justify their subject on the grounds that knowledge of the classical languages helps children learn English. In *Curriculum Matters 12*, for example, it is argued that 'an awareness of the classical origins of many English words can begin in the primary school and should be available to all' (DES 1988: 6); Peter Jones, putting the case for the classical languages in the QCA publication *Classics in the Curriculum*, goes further than word derivations and argues that 'by learning how a language quite different from English functions, we get a much better grasp of the workings of English' (Jones 1997: 6); and Barbara Bell, discussing the place of *Minimus*,

---

[10] 'Raising the flag again', *Times Educational Supplement*, 15 June 2001.

her primary school Latin course, in the National Curriculum, says that '*Minimus* is about teaching English grammar – parts of speech, word derivations, prefixes, suffixes etc. – through simple Latin' (Bell 2003: 63), and cites the headteacher of a primary school in Kent using *Minimus* in the literacy hour who said that it offered 'splendid material for Word, Sentence and Text Levels, as well as for etymology, an important part of the work in Literacy' (Bell 2003: 65).[11]

One nevertheless needs to sound a word of caution about the use of Latin to support the learning of English grammar as a way to secure a firm footing for classics in the primary curriculum, since the link between Latin and English is not appreciated by everyone: in his major review of research relating to the NLS, Roger Beard notes that 'there is evidence that in recent years explicit use of grammatical terms has been less evident in schools because of a dissatisfaction with the Latin model on which older approaches to grammar teaching were based' (Beard 2000: 49). Even among those who believe that Latin can help pupils' English, few people, including classicists, argue that it would be appropriate to offer Latin to the full ability range at primary level, and unless that were the case it would never be included as an integral part of the primary curriculum. In spite of the fact that *Minimus* is being used in perhaps 10 per cent of primary schools, Barbara Bell admits 'it would be living in Cloudcuckooland to hope for Latin as a National Curriculum subject' (Bell 2003: 66).

Another possible way to exploit the current emphasis on grammar teaching would be to develop a Key Stage 2 language awareness course to complement the NLS, along the lines of Adrian Spooner's *Lingo*, teaching principles of word building and sentence structure within a framework of stories in English from classical mythology. It would be much easier to design a language awareness than a Latin course for the full ability range but as James Morwood notes, discussing curriculum developments in classics that 'have promised much but delivered less': 'language awareness failed to secure a significant foothold in the school curriculum' (Morwood 2003: xix). Writing in 1990 when language awareness courses were being promoted as a possible way to help keep classics in state schools, Richard Woff warned about making exaggerated claims about their potential benefits:

> While I think that language awareness is basically a Good Thing, I also think that we must be very careful about what claims are made for it ... I believe that at present we both make too strong a

---

[11] This example of Latin in primary schools was particularly encouraging because although the headteacher's initial intention had been to use *Minimus* with children on their gifted and talented programme, she decided to use it with the full ability range.

case for what language awareness courses based in classics can do and at the same time are in danger of offering an impoverished form of language awareness to our pupils.

(Woff 1990: 3)

He examined in particular etymology and the extent to which language awareness courses could claim to advance the development of children's vocabulary. Drawing on Corson's work (e.g. Corson 1982 and Corson 1985), he argued that while classical language awareness courses might help extend pupils' passive vocabulary (i.e. 'words one tends to use only infrequently or in very particular circumstances and words which are familiar, but not understood well enough to be used actively' (Woff 1990: 4), they did nothing to shift words from the reservoir of a pupil's passive vocabulary into the mainstream of their active vocabulary. He also had a general point to make about teaching etymology: 'no matter how interesting one may try to make etymology, only words are being made the focus of the students' attention. In etymology lessons the students are inundated with unfamiliar words which have been torn from any context.' He concluded that a classical studies course that provided a meaningful context for children to grapple with important issues was much more likely than a language awareness course to promote active use of Graeco-Latin lexis.

Whether one thinks in terms of Latin or language awareness courses for primary schools, the fundamental problem with linking classics too closely to the teaching of English grammar is that among English specialists there are serious reservations about the prominence given to it in the NLS. A key argument for introducing more explicit teaching of grammar was that it would lead to improved standards in written work, but according to critics (e.g. Wyse 2006) there is no research evidence to support this claim. Wyse quotes the work of Constance Weaver who, after conducting a thorough review of research on grammar from a historical perspective, concluded that

> these three studies [reviewed in depth] as well as numerous others during the twentieth century indicate that there is little pragmatic justification for systematically teaching a descriptive or explanatory grammar of the language, whether that grammar be traditional, structural, transformational, or any other kind.
>
> (Weaver 1996: 23; cited in Wyse 2006: 34)

Even Roger Beard, a strong supporter of the NLS, admitted in a major research review that 'research reviews (e.g. Wilkinson 1971) have consistently failed to provide evidence that grammar teaching makes any difference to the quality of children's writing' (Beard

2000: 49). More recently a group of leading children's writers put together a collection of short essays, *Waiting for a Jamie Oliver: Beyond Bog-Standard Literacy*, in which they challenged the approach to language adopted by the NLS on a number of grounds. Philip Pullman, for example, argued that before children start working on grammar something more basic has to be in place, 'an attitude to the language, to work, to the world itself ... The study of grammar is intensely fascinating; but only when [children are] ready for it' (Pullman 2005: 8–9). Underlying all the writers' concerns was a fundamental disagreement with the model of literacy underpinning the NLS, summed up by Chris Powling in the opening essay:

> It is hardly a revelation that there are two competing ways to conceptualise literacy:
>
> - as a skill-based activity which demands discipline, practice and repetition
> - as a means of making the world meaningful ... with motivation and appropriate materials at a premium.
>
> As professional writers, we recognise the validity and the necessity of both approaches (though not necessarily in that order). If only the National Literacy Strategy did the same. Its relentless prioritising of the first, by way of drilling and testing and 'texts' has so undermined the second that bog-standard literacy is now not only the norm but presented as some kind of success story.
>
> (Powling 2005: 6)

The *Framework* defines literacy as 'communication skill. The term literacy originally, and most often, applied to written communication; however, it can also be applied to other forms, as in media literacy, computer literacy' (DfEE 1998: 82). This narrow definition of literacy, with the emphasis firmly on written communication, has given rise, as Powling notes, to a regime of drilling and testing in many schools, with teachers resorting to formulaic teaching methods in order to ensure that their pupils perform well in the Year 6 Standard Assessment Tasks (SATs). This was picked up by Ofsted in their most recent review of research evidence on the teaching of English: they observed that while the NLS had brought improvements in teaching, such as more precise learning objectives, 'some teachers are using the learning objects from the *Framework* inflexibly, seeing them as a set of requirements to be ticked off and, as a result, learning does not match the particular needs of the pupils in the class' (Ofsted 2005c: 6).

Classics and literature

Turning from the teaching of language to the teaching of literature, we find a strong link, as noted earlier, between classics and English at Key Stage 2 (DfEE/QCA 1999a: 26), where myths and legends are part of the required reading (along with modern fiction by significant children's authors, long-established children's fiction, good-quality modern poetry, classic poetry and playscripts) to be covered over the four years of Key Stage 2. This offers a clear opportunity for a substantial unit of work on Greek mythology,[12] perhaps as part of a term-long exploration of traditional stories, from fairy tales through to the Homeric epics.

Such a mythology unit must incorporate the learning objectives for literature at Key Stage 2, both those specified in the standing orders and those specified in the *Framework*. The standing orders for English require that pupils at Key Stage 2 should be taught to

a recognise the choice, use and effect of figurative language, vocabulary and patterns of language

b identify different ways of constructing sentences and their effects

c identify how character and setting are created, and how plot, narrative structure and themes are developed

d recognise the differences between author, narrator and character

e evaluate ideas and themes that broaden perspectives and extend thinking

f consider poetic forms and their effects

g express preferences and support their views by reference to texts

h respond imaginatively, drawing on the whole text and other reading

i read stories, poems and plays aloud.

(DfEE/QCA 1999a: 26)

This is an ambitious set of objectives, and many secondary school teachers who teach classical literature at GCSE, whether in the original or in translation, might feel that relatively few of their pupils are likely to have met these objectives by the time they enter Year 10, let alone by the end of Year 6. If pupils are going to develop their understanding and appreciation of literary texts through stories from

---

[12] It would also be possible to include stories from Roman mythology, but because Greek myths and legends are also included in the Key Stage 2 history requirements, I focus only on Greek mythology in this discussion.

Greek mythology, careful thought must be given to the selection of myths and the form in which pupils encounter them. This was particularly the case when each school could choose when, during the four years of Key Stage 2, to cover myths and legends, but the situation has been made easier with the introduction of the *Framework*, which specifies that myths and legends should be read in Year 5 Term 2. The reading comprehension objectives for Year 5 Term 2 are:

Pupils should be taught

1 to identify and classify the features of myths, legends and fables, e.g. the moral in a fable, fantastical beasts in legends;

2 to investigate different versions of the same story in print or on film, identifying similarities and differences; recognise how stories change over time and differences of culture and place that are expressed in stories;

3 to explore similarities and differences between oral and written story telling;

4 to read a range of narrative poems;

5 to perform poems in a variety of ways;

6 to understand terms which describe different kinds of poems, e.g. ballad, sonnet, rap, elegy, narrative poem, and to identify typical features;

7 to compile a class anthology of favourite poems with commentaries which illuminate the choice;

8 to distinguish between the author and the narrator, investigating narrative viewpoint and the treatment of different characters, e.g. minor characters, heroes, villains, and perspectives on the action from different characters;

9 to investigate the features of different fiction genres, e.g. science fiction, adventure, discussing the appeal of popular fiction;

10 to understand the differences between literal and figurative language, e.g. through discussing the effects of imagery in poetry and prose.

(DfEE 1998: 46)

These objectives strengthen the case for promoting Greek mythology as the topic most likely to secure the place of classics in the primary curriculum. While neither the standing orders for English nor the *Framework for Teaching* specify from which culture(s) the myths and legends should be drawn, no single corpus of stories better enables a teacher to cover these objectives than Greek mythology: it encompasses the full range of story types identified in objective 1;

the stories are available in a wide range of media, providing ample opportunity for comparing different versions (objective 2), and, in particular, for comparing oral and written story telling (objective 3); and it includes the greatest narrative poems in western literature (objective 4), poems which provide ample scope for discussing literal and figurative language (objective 10). In short, the general thrust of the NLS Year 5 Term 2 objectives gives ample encouragement to teach not just shorter stories such as Demeter and Persephone or Daedalus and Icarus, but also longer adventures such as the story of Theseus or the Homeric epics.

Although the *Iliad* and the *Odyssey* provide the richest opportunity for developing pupils' understanding and appreciation of literature, there is a potential drawback in placing too much emphasis on these long narrative poems: primary school teachers may well be put off by the sheer scale of the poems, particularly as many are anyway unwilling to read whole texts with classes, preferring to use extracts instead as a more efficient way to address word and sentence level learning objectives (because these are what the English SATs test):

> Many of us [here] have been witness to the fact that the way books are read in schools has, over the last four or five years, changed. We are full of anecdotal evidence of, say, years 5 and 6 classrooms where whole books are *not being read*; where books are being chopped up into fragments which are then turned into worksheets; and these fragments are then used as examples on spotting verbs and similes.
>
> (Rosen 2005: 13)

And where they do use whole texts, according to Ofsted's most recent review of English teaching:

> Teachers often make use of texts without adequately considering their impact upon the pupils. They appear to regard texts primarily as a means of teaching writing: a poem is mined for its use of adjectives, metaphors and contrasting short and long sentences without attempting to engage pupils' personal response to the ideas and feelings it expresses. The text becomes a kind of manual rather than an opportunity for personal response to experience.
>
> (Ofsted 2005c: 23)

This raises fundamental questions about the balance between the teaching of language and the teaching of literature in the NLS. For one academic the style and presentation of the NLS make it clear which has priority:

The 'common language' of the *Framework* ... privileges a literacy curriculum in which the study of the formal structures of language and the achievement of organisational textual skills are central. Through the authoritative instructional style of the *Framework*, the 'common language' thus represents literacy in objective, tabular terms and as value-free and straightforward to describe, teach and measure. What is harder to assess, and thus harder to include in the 'common language', are the wider but less quantifiable purposes, the more literary, moral and emotional consequences of becoming a competent and discriminating reader and writer. These wider purposes involve reference to difficult and ambiguous ideas, such as *joy, creativity* and *meaning*, and acknowledge the importance of a professional understanding of what makes children want to read and write, what engages them about texts that they read and that adults read with them and inspires them to want to write as powerfully as the authors they have encountered.

(Urquhart 2002: 31)

One can understand why it is felt essential to teach children to read before introducing them to literature: many people would regard it as self-evident that a basic reading competence must precede engagement with literature – the underlying assumption is that literature must be *read*. But a key aspect of myths and legends, the *Iliad* and the *Odyssey* in particular, is that they are products of an oral tradition and lend themselves naturally to storytelling which, by removing the barrier of the printed word, enables non-readers and reluctant readers to respond to, engage with and talk about stories on an equal footing with classmates who are already fluent readers. We shall see evidence of this in chapter 4 when we look at an evaluation of *War with Troy* as a classroom resource, but first we shall look at the place of myths and storytelling in classical education over the last forty years.

References

Bage, G., Grisdale, R. and Lister, B. (1999). *The Ancient Greeks and Romans in Primary Schools: An Evaluation*. London, QCA

Beard, R. (2000). *National Literacy Strategy: Review of Research and Other Related Evidence*. London: DfEE

Bell, B. (2003). 'Minimus', in Morwood, J. (ed.), *The Teaching of Classics*. Cambridge: Cambridge University Press

Corson, D. (1982). 'The Graeco-Latin lexical bar', *Hesperiam* 5, pp. 49–59

Corson, D. (1985). *The Lexical Bar*. Oxford: Pergamon Press

Cowen, R. (1992). *A Study of the Ancient Greeks with Upper Juniors*. Cambridge: Cambridge School Classics Project

DES (1985). *The curriculum from 5 to 16, Curriculum Matters 2*. London: HMSO

DES (1988). *Classics from 5 to 16, Curriculum Matters 12*. London: HMSO

DfEE (1998). *The National Literacy Strategy: A Framework for Teaching*. London: DfEE

DfEE (2000). *The National Literacy Strategy: Grammar for Writing*. London: DfEE

DfEE/QCA (1999a). *The National Curriculum for England: English*. London: HMSO

DfEE/QCA (1999b). *The National Curriculum for England: History*. London: HMSO

Farrell, J. and Forrest, M. (1989). *Classics in the Primary School: A Pilot Study during 1986–7*. Cambridge: Cambridge School Classics Project

Gay, B. (2003). 'Classics teaching and the National Curriculum', in Morwood, J. (ed.), *The Teaching of Classics*. Cambridge: Cambridge University Press

Jones, P. (1997). 'The rationale for classics', in QCA, *Classics in the Curriculum*. London: QCA

Morwood, J. (ed.) (2003). *The Teaching of Classics*. Cambridge: Cambridge University Press

Ofsted (2005a). *The Annual Report of Her Majesty's Chief Inspector of Schools, 2004/05*. Retrieved on 1 November 2006 from http://live.ofsted.gov.uk/publications/annualreport0405/annual_report.html

Ofsted (2005b). Ofsted subject reports 2003/04: history in primary schools. Retrieved on 1 November 2006 from http://live.ofsted.gov.uk/publications/annualreport0304/subject_reports/primary/history.htm

Ofsted (2005c). *English 2000–05: A Review of Inspection Evidence*. London: Ofsted

Powling, C. (2005). 'Bog-standard literacy', in Powling, C. (ed.), *Waiting for a Jamie Oliver: Beyond Bog-Standard Literacy*. Reading: National Centre for Language and Literacy

Pullman, P. (2005). 'Common sense has much to learn from moonshine', in Powling, C. (ed.), *Waiting for a Jamie Oliver: Beyond Bog-Standard Literacy*. Reading: National Centre for Language and Literacy

QCA (2005). *History: 2004/5 Annual Report on Curriculum and Assessment*. London: QCA

Rosen, M. (2005). 'Children's reading', in Powling, C. (ed.), *Waiting for a Jamie Oliver: Beyond Bog-Standard Literacy*. Reading: National Centre for Language and Literacy

Sharwood Smith, J. E. (1977). *On Teaching Classics*. London: Routledge and Kegan Paul

Urquhart, I. (2002). 'Moving forward together: do we need a "common language"?' *Cambridge Journal of Education* 32(1), pp. 27–44

Weaver, C. (1996). *Teaching Grammar in Context*. Portsmouth, New Hampshire: Heinemann

Wilkinson, A. (1971). *The Foundations of Language: Talking and Reading in Young Children*. Oxford: Oxford University Press

Woff, R. (1990). 'L.A. Lore', *JACT Review* 2(8), pp. 4–7

Woff, R. (2003). 'Classics and museums', in Morwood, J. (ed.), *The Teaching of Classics*. Cambridge: Cambridge University Press

Wyse, D. (2006). 'Pupils' word choices and the teaching of grammar', *Cambridge Journal of Education* 36(1), pp. 31–47

3 Myths and legends in the classroom

Writing in *Crisis in the Humanities* in 1964, Moses Finley observed that 'it is paradoxical that formal education should be in such danger precisely at a time when popular interest in classical literature, art, and archaeology is far greater than ever before. That not only lends poignancy to the crisis; it also seems to hold out hope that all may not be lost' (Finley 1964: 12). When classicists are seeking reassurance about the value and importance of their subject, they often take comfort in this popular interest in the classical world, even though it may be a reaction, at least in part, to the limited access to classics in school. In recent years the continuing appeal of classics has been evident in films like *Gladiator* and *Troy*; television programmes like *Rome*; in books such as Margaret Atwood's *The Penelopiad* and Peter Ackroyd's *The Fall of Troy*, Robert Harris's *Pompeii* and *Imperium*, and Lindsey Davies's Marcus Didius Falco mysteries; in poetry such as Derek Walcott's *Omeros* and Ted Hughes's *Tales from Ovid*; and in any number of new theatre productions of Greek plays or plays based on classical originals. Writers and artists are constantly finding messages for the modern world in the stories of the ancient world: a personal favourite is Steven Sherrill's *The Minotaur Takes a Cigarette Break*, in which the Minotaur is cast as a chef working in a diner in the Deep South, who struggles with personal relationships and the practicalities of daily life when you have horns.

Popular interest in classical literature can be traced back to the middle of the last century, when it first became available in a range of different translations written with the non-specialist in mind. W. H. D. Rouse may have complained in his introduction to *The Story of Odysseus* about the lack of translations of Homer 'free from affectations and attempts at poetic language which Homer himself is quite free from' (Rieu 1937: vii); but this gap was quickly filled after the Second World War with the publication of E. V. Rieu's translation of the *Odyssey*, shortly followed by the *Iliad*, in the Penguin Classics series (which Rieu himself edited from 1944 to 1964), and since then new translations have appeared at regular intervals. In his introduction to *Homer in English*, George Steiner reckons that English-language 'Homers' decisively outnumber English renditions of the Bible and goes on to claim that:

> the 'translation act' which renders the Trojan War, the homecoming of Odysseus or the Homeric Hymns into medieval, Tudor, Elizabethan, Jacobean, Augustan, Romantic, Victorian or twentieth-century English, into the English of North America or the Caribbean, surpasses in frequency that of any other act of transfer into any other Western tongue and literature.
>
> (Steiner 1996: xv–xvi)

Children and mythology

This popularity has been equally evident in children's literature. Classical mythology is, not surprisingly, a strong source of inspiration for children's writers, and has been for more than 150 years. The American writer, Nathaniel Hawthorne, whose collection of classical myths, *Tanglewood Tales*, was first published in 1853, opens the preface of my English edition with the assertion that he 'has long been of opinion that many of the classical myths were capable of being rendered into very capital reading for children', and goes on to say,

> No epoch of time can claim a copyright in these immortal fables. They seem never to have been made; and certainly, so long as man exists, they can never perish; but, by their indestructibility itself, they are legitimate subjects for every age to clothe with its own garniture of manners and sentiment, and to imbue with its own morality.

During the last hundred years, children's writers have again and again reworked stories from the classical world. If we look, for instance, at some of the adaptations of the Homeric epics for children, Andrew Lang's *Tales of Troy and Greece* was published in 1907; W. H. D. Rouse's *The Story of Odysseus* came out in 1937; Roger Lancelyn Green's *The Tale of Troy* (1958) was for many years used as a standard text in classical studies foundation courses; and in the last ten years Rosemary Sutcliff's posthumously published *Black Ships before Troy* (1993) and *The Wanderings of Odysseus* (1995), with illustrations by Alan Lee, have become established as the best modern adaptations of the *Iliad* and the *Odyssey* for children. There are also more lighthearted versions, such as Tony Robinson and Richard Curtis's *Odysseus: the Greatest Hero of Them All*, available in both book and audio-cassette format; a comic strip version of the *Odyssey* by Diane Redmond and Robin Kingsland;[1] and a young children's picture book, *'The Iliad' and 'The Odyssey'*, by Marcia Williams, covering the story of the two epics in thirty-two pages. There have also been a number of very good historical novels based on Greek mythology over the last forty years: in the 1960s, Ian Serraillier wrote *The Way of Danger* (based on the adventures of Theseus) and *The Clashing Rocks* (based on the story of Jason); in the 1970s Leon Garfield and Edward Blishen brought out *The God beneath the Sea* and *The Golden Shadow*, with haunting illustrations by Charles Keeping; and more recently Adèle Geras has given us the *Iliad* and the *Odyssey* from a girl's perspective, with *Troy* (2000) and *Ithaka* (2005).

The evidence from the GRIPS report discussed in the previous chapter showed that myths and legends were popular in the classroom, and in this chapter we look at the value of Greek mythology as a creative stimulus in a mixed ability classroom and consider the importance of storytelling as a medium for introducing children to myths and legends, including the Homeric epics. Relatively few children now experience the intimacy, enjoyment and excitement that come from having a story told to them, in the manner Jean-Pierre Vernant describes entertaining his grandson:

> A quarter century ago, when my grandson was a child and spent his vacations with my wife and me, one routine came to be as imperative as bathing and meals: Every evening, when the time came for Julien to go to bed, I would hear him call to me from his room, often rather impatiently: 'J.-P. – the story! The story!' I would go sit beside him and tell him some Greek legend. It was no trouble for me to pull something out of my repertory of myths that I spent my professional time analyzing, dissecting, comparing, and interpreting as I worked to understand them, but that I passed along to him in another way – straight out, however they came to me, like a fairy tale. My only concern was to follow the thread of the story from start to finish holding on to its dramatic tension: 'Once upon a time ...' Julien was all ears, and looked happy. I was, too. I took delight in passing on to him straight from my mouth to his ear a little of that Greek universe for which I care so much.
>
> (Vernant 2001: viii–ix)

---

[1] Eric Shanower started an ambitious comic strip version of the *Iliad* for adults, *Age of Bronze*, which was published in instalments in the States, but it ground to a halt, I believe, with the sacrifice of Iphigeneia at Aulis.

First, however, it will be helpful to consider the best age for introducing mythology in schools and the extent to which mythology can be taught to the full ability range. The answer to the first question has, to an extent, been rendered redundant by the introduction of the National Curriculum, which, as we have seen, places myths and legends firmly in Key Stage 2 of the primary curriculum. This is as Elizabeth Cook would have wanted: in *The Ordinary and the Fabulous* (which remains the standard work on teaching myths and legends) she states that 'there is a hard, alert, often cheerful objectivity in the way in which most [myths] were told in antiquity [which is] congenial to children between the ages of 8 and 11' (Cook 1969: 10; cited in DES 1988: 12). In *Curriculum Matters 12* HMI broadly supported Elizabeth Cook's point of view, though they advised that 'it is impossible to stipulate a precise age at which this material should be introduced' (DES 1988: 12–13), and rightly pointed out that not all stories were equally suitable for younger children. With regard to the *Iliad* specifically, HMI included the legends of Troy in their corpus of stories appropriate for younger children (along with Orpheus and Eurydice, Theseus and the Minotaur, Demeter and Persephone, Atlanta, and Zeus and Prometheus), whereas Elizabeth Cook wanted to leave the *Iliad* ('the most complex of Greek heroic legends') until later, stating categorically, 'it is a story for the years between eleven and fourteen, and cannot be told earlier, even with skilful cutting' (Cook 1969: 21). But her concern that the story is too long and complex for younger listeners is misplaced: children relish the scale and intricacy of longer stories, provided they are pitched at the right level, and have a strong narrative thread and engaging characters. One has only to think of the popularity of *Lord of the Rings* and *Harry Potter*, which have been highly successful both as books and as films.

Myths and inclusion

The case for teaching myths to eleven- to fourteen-year-olds had been put forward earlier in *Humanities for the Young School Leaver: an Approach through Classics* (Schools Council 1967). This report, written in response to the raising of the school leaving age and the expansion of comprehensive schools, was one of the earliest government publications to propose a classics course 'which would be much wider than the traditional study of Latin, Greek and ancient history, and which could be taken by pupils of a wider range of ability' (Schools Council 1967: 3). It provided two examples of courses that demonstrated how classics could be integrated into a broader humanities programme and showed that such courses could offer challenges for the full ability range.

The first example was taken from a grammar school, which ran a highly ambitious three-year course designed to teach 'the development of the earth and its people as science tells us' as a contrast to 'the poetic account of the Bible' (Schools Council 1967: 10). It was based on an overview of world history and culture from the civilisations of Egypt and Assyria through to the Renaissance. Most of the first year (Year 7), which began with great inventions like the wheel and the lever, and the discovery of fire (when the story of Prometheus was taught), was taken up with the stories and history of the Greeks, beginning with the adventures of the Argonauts ('the first great exploration'), partly told and partly read, using excerpts from Apollonius Rhodius, going on to the stories of Hercules, Perseus and Oedipus, and ending with the Homeric epics. During the course pupils undertook a range of predominantly written activities, and their responses to the stories matched the high demands of the course:

> Pupils very soon absorb Homeric style and diction, his similes, stock epithets etc., and with little encouragement from the teacher try to imitate them in their own written work based on the material read. The Iliad gives plenty of scope for this, e.g. a speech in the Trojan assembly for or against the return of Helen, an account of a patrol against the enemy told by a Trojan or an Achaean, Hector's death described by an onlooker, or the description of a tapestry depicting this scene (in imitation of the Shield of Achilles).
>
> (Schools Council 1967: 11–12)

The second example was of a humanities course in a secondary modern school, which was based loosely on the grammar school programme described above. The second year (Year 8) of the course was described as follows:

> In the second year, when Greek civilisation and literature in translation is studied, the myth is the starting point from which much that is creative seems naturally to flow. The telling of shorter stories, the reading of the longer legends – including the great epics of the *Iliad* and the *Odyssey* – evoke this response from *even the simplest child* [emphasis added], perhaps because the literature itself stems from a simple folk-lore.
>
> These stories find expression in countless ways, spontaneous dramatisation, pictorial illustration etc.; and with the brighter pupils, narration in verse form or the writing of short plays or scenes.

... The wanderings of Odysseus and his encounters with enchantress and monster are followed with great enjoyment by the pupils at all levels and result in written work of a high standard by the brighter girls. Those not so well equipped for written work find their outlet in other creative channels – for example, a model has been made by them in papier maché, showing all the phases of Odysseus' journey.

(Schools Council 1967: 25–6)

Leaving aside the dubious connection between simple children and simple literature, the underlying point remains, that myths and legends have something to offer low-achieving (and, one might add, disaffected) pupils as well as motivated, high-achieving pupils. I saw this for myself as a trainee teacher on my main school placement in a mixed comprehensive in east London, formed from the amalgamation of two single-sex secondary modern schools. In this challenging environment where less than 5 per cent of pupils stayed on in the sixth form, classical studies was taught to all pupils in Year 7, following a course not unlike that in the secondary modern above, entirely devoted to Greek mythology. The key element of every lesson was a dramatic retelling of a myth. I can still remember observing a Year 7 class listening to a particularly gory retelling of the Tantalus story. At the key moment a rather quiet boy was brought to the front of the class to take on the hapless role of Pelops. The teacher expertly butchered the boy on the desk at the front, and then, with anxious glances now and then to check if the gods were on their way, kept stirring his giant cooking pot to make sure no meat stuck to the bottom, adding plenty of seasoning to conceal the real contents of his stew. Finally he described the meal, Artemis' instant recognition of human flesh and the gods' compassionate reconstructive surgery, including an ivory shoulder replacement. And Tantalus' fate? Like all good soap operas, that was left for the following week. The pupils were hooked: they looked forward to every lesson and their enthusiasm and motivation was evident in the wide range of responses to the stories.

The extent to which myths and legends can be used as an inclusive resource was clearly demonstrated on a visit to a school for children with profound and multiple learning difficulties, where I observed a teacher telling the story of Theseus and the Minotaur to a Year 7 group of six children. All but one of the children were working at P level 1 or 2, and were unable to follow the logical sequence of even the simplest story.[2] But using a mixture of

---

[2] P levels are levels of attainment leading up to National Curriculum level 1 and are designed specifically to describe the types and range of general performance demonstrated by pupils with learning difficulties. For instance, pupils working at level P2i 'begin to

PowerPoint presentation, dramatic re-enactment (for the fight in the labyrinth), tape-recorded music and physical effects (for instance, spraying the children with water as Theseus crossed the Aegean), the teacher created a multisensory experience that she felt triggered an affective response in her pupils.

Her approach was based directly on the pioneering work of Nicola Grove and Keith Park, the authors of *Odyssey Now*, a dramatisation incorporating a variety of interactive games, accompanied by music and slides, designed for people with severe learning difficulties. Their belief is that everyone, regardless of disability, has the capacity to come to know and enjoy the stories, art and music that form their cultural heritage:

> How necessary is verbal comprehension to the understanding of poetry and literature? Do we have to *comprehend* before we can *apprehend*? Does the 'meaning' of a poem or story have to be retrieved through a process of decoding individual words, or can it be grasped through a kind of atmosphere created through sound and vision? We would like to suggest that all of us derive enjoyment from hearing music and poetry, and seeing pictures, often without being very sure what they 'mean'.
>
> (Grove and Park 1996: 2)

Elsewhere Nicola Grove goes on to argue that a person's response to literature and art is both emotional and intellectual, and that 'our ability to evaluate a work of art is dependent on our ability to engage with it at a physical and an emotional level' (Grove 2005: 3). Whether or not one accepts that children *must* respond to literature at an emotional level before they are able to engage with it at an analytical level, there are many who would argue that if we are to promote the reading of literature as an enjoyable pastime, the emphasis in the classroom must be on emotional engagement before critical analysis. This point was made over 160 years ago by A. W. Kinglake in *Eothen*:

> A learned commentator knows something of the Greeks, in the same sense as an oil and colour-man may be said to know something of painting; but take an untamed child, and leave him alone for twelve months with any translation of Homer, and he will be nearer by twenty centuries to the spirit of old Greece; he does not stop in the ninth year of the siege to admire this or that group of words – he has no books in his tent, but he shares in vital

---

respond consistently to familiar people, events and objects. React to new shared activities and experiences, for example, withholding their attention. Begin to show interest in people, events and objects, for example smiling at familiar people. Accept and engage in coactive exploration, for example focusing their attention on sensory aspects of stories or rhymes when prompted' (DfES 2002: 7).

counsels with the 'King of Men', and knows the inmost souls of the impending Gods; how profanely he exults over the powers divine, when they are taught to dread the prowess of mortals! and most of all how he rejoices when the God of War flies howling from the spear of Diomed, and mounts into heaven for safety! Then the beautiful episode of the 6th book: the way to feel this is not to go casting about, and learning from pastors and masters, how best to admire it; the impatient child is not grubbing for beauties, but pushing the siege; the women vex him with their delays, and their talking – the mention of the nurse is personal, and little sympathy has he for the child that is young enough to be frightened by the nodding plume of a helmet.

(Kinglake 1982: 30)[3]

Myths and story-centred teaching

The publication by the Schools Council in 1967 of *Humanities for the Young School Leaver: An Approach through Classics* marked the beginning of a golden era in the teaching of classical studies foundation courses (they were known as 'foundation' courses because they were designed to lead on to the learning of Latin). At the beginning of that year Martin Forrest had joined the Cambridge School Classics Project (CSCP) on a full-time post with particular responsibility for developing non-linguistic classical courses. He advocated a story-centred approach to such courses, with stories used as a springboard for a range of creative activities and as a starting point for further research. Discovering that there was a serious shortage of appropriate books and resources to support such an approach, and drawing on his own experience of using the 'Jackdaw' series of history folders, he began development of equivalent resource packs for classical stories. These contained photographs, line drawings and written texts and were designed for the very wide range of ability that was to be found in the growing number of comprehensive schools.[4] Although he started with a trial group of only five schools in 1967, by the time formal trials of the resource folders began in 1968, sixty schools were taking part and this number quickly rose to more than a hundred.

After successful completion of the trials the revised materials were published as the Greek World Foundation Course, comprising five folders[5] and a Teacher's Handbook, which set out the rationale for the course, gave practical advice on choosing and presenting

---

[3] *Eothen* was first published in 1844.
[4] For a full account of CSCP's Classical Studies foundation course, see Forrest (1996), chapter 6.
[5] The five folders, published by Cambridge University Press, were Troy and the Early Greeks; The Gods of Mount Olympus; Greek Religion; Athens, Sparta and Persia; and Greek Festivals.

stories and provided complete programmes of work. Even as the folders were being prepared for publication CSCP began a sustained programme of dissemination and soon schools 'stretching from Stornaway to Penzance' (Forrest 1996: 88) were using the materials. A national survey of comprehensive schools by HMI (DES 1977: 8) gave some indication of the extent to which these new foundation courses took root in schools. It showed that in 1974 (when the survey was undertaken) seventy-three (24 per cent) of a random sample of 309 comprehensive schools offered some form of classical studies course, in most cases (sixty-three schools) as a foundation course leading on to Latin. Acknowledging CSCP's pioneering work, HMI commended the story-centred approach

(i) for its attempt, often successful, to use material appropriate to the pupil's level of experience and sophistication: the myths, which naturally incorporate unrealistic elements recognisable as such by the children, are frequently fascinating and challenging for pupils in this age group;

(ii) for the flexibility it provides: this is important in teaching groups which are likely to have a widespread of literacy and intellectual ability (and useful when pupils are fresh from primary schools), and there can be some adjustment of rational and imaginative content;

(iii) for the range of activities made possible, depending upon accommodation and resources.

(DES 1977: 51)

Looking at the material and articles written in the late 1960s and early 1970s, one is struck by the creativity and imagination – and optimism too – of contributors. This is evident, for instance, in the worksheets and lesson plans available through the London Association of Classical Teachers (LACT) foundation course bureau (its existence is itself proof of the healthy state of classical studies), run by Malcolm Young, who worked closely with Martin Forrest. Discussing a lesson on the shield of Achilles, a teacher from a boys' grammar school described his own approach:

After reading [Homer's account], I ask the class what they notice about the description. It takes several comments to get to what always strikes me as the most obvious fact – that the shield is a movie with sound effects – i.e. that Homer's imagination has run away with itself. But once this fact dawns ... there is quite a bit of fun. I ask them to try to think of ways in which Hephaestus' effects might be achieved (the field of gold turning black, for instance); and what the size of the shield might have to be to accommodate all the scenes. In fact, I just let ideas go as they will (Would Homer have made a good film-director? How important is it that Hephaestus is a god in Homer's mind? Had Homer seen anything at all like this? What were the shields like in those days? What size would the figures have to be to fit on to a shield of, say, six feet diameter at the most?)

Another LACT resource, from a comprehensive school teacher in Sunderland, provided a planning diagram for teaching the judgement of Paris through a story-centred approach, as shown in figure 1.

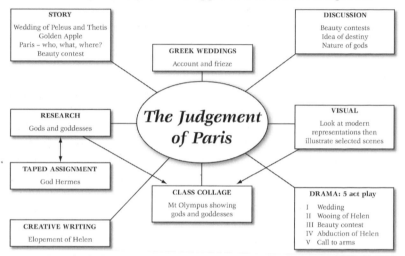

Figure 1 *LACT planning diagram for teaching the judgement of Paris*

The story-centred approach presupposed a generous time allocation (imagine how long it would take to teach all aspects of the judgement of Paris following the scheme above), which was made possible by integrating classical studies in a broader humanities course; and in the hands of a skilled practitioner it provided a challenging and stimulating learning experience for a wide range of pupils. In the hands of a dull or unimaginative teacher, on the other hand, such lessons could be depressingly formulaic, as John Sharwood Smith graphically described:

> Teacher tells one of the hackneyed stories – say Theseus and the Minotaur – known already to half the children from their primary school days, then asks them a few questions to make sure they have been listening; after that he tells them to disperse into groups and paint the Minotaur, or write a playlet about the elopement of Theseus and Ariadne, or make a plasticine model of the labyrinth, or a tape-recorded account of an afternoon in the

bull-ring, or write the front-page of the 'Minoan Times' for the day after the earthquake – and stay out of trouble until the end of the double lesson.

(Sharwood Smith 1977: 14)

This is a timely reminder that good stories alone do not make successful lessons. Nor are good stories of themselves accessible to the full ability range: they require effective mediation by the teacher; and the younger the pupils, the less confident the readers and the wider the ability span, the more important the role of the teacher is. In the challenging case of a special school, the teacher needs the imagination, resourcefulness and determination of a latter-day Odysseus to bring the story to life for her pupils.

Myths and storytelling

Above all the success of a myth lesson depends on the actual method of transmission. This was forcefully argued by Steve Woodward in an article in *Hesperiam* describing the teaching of myth in Dinnington Comprehensive School in South Yorkshire, where the classical studies course focused on myth and drama and was based on the premise that there is a uniqueness in the progression from myth to drama, reflected in the fact that 'Greek tragedy has as its basis the whole body of Greek myth' (Woodward 1980: 37). Steve Woodward was clear that the success of dramatic enactments by pupils was directly related to the quality of the initial telling by the teacher:

> It is, of course, quite possible to issue duplicated sheets or textbooks that contain versions of Greek myths and from either reading these to the class or having the class read them silently to themselves to develop dramatic enactments. This method works; it works, however, on only a *limited* level and is best used as a variation from the central method. This central method is the method of telling a story directly to an audience without reference to a text. The reason why this method is more effective is quite simply that the teacher is forced in his role as story-teller to devise dramatic ways of presenting the myth, which in turn elicit the dramatic responses of the individuals in the audience. No straight reading from a book ever achieves quite the same effect.

(Woodward 1980: 37–8)

While I share Woodward's belief that storytelling is the best method of transmission (not least because of my experiences as a trainee listening to the story of Tantalus), I am less ready to accept that a silent reading of a myth is an effective stimulus for drama enactments or, indeed, any other type of creative activity. For most children, even at Year 8 or 9, the printed word creates a significant barrier between themselves and the story, not only because of difficulties they may have with basic decoding, but also because they find it hard to build up sufficient momentum in their reading to keep hold of the narrative thread, especially when the story includes unfamiliar vocabulary and strange-sounding names. Even relatively confident and fluent readers find that the demands of reading detract from the pleasure of engaging with the story. A surprising number of teachers, however, seem nervous about taking on the role of storyteller, even though storytelling is only an extension of their everyday classroom 'performance'. In many cases their anxiety is caused in part by fear of forgetting the story and drying up in front of the class. This stems from a misunderstanding of what storytelling involves: it is not the repetition of a text learnt by heart, but the improvised colouring-in of a story familiar in outline or, more accurately, the detailed description of a tightly connected sequence of tableaux. A simple but very effective way to prepare a story for telling is to create a story-board (in exactly the same way as one might later ask a class to create a story-board), focusing on the key scenes and characters.[6] This, as we shall see in the next chapter, is the approach adopted by the storytellers on the Iliad Project.

For teachers unwilling to tell stories without a script, reading a story aloud is still a much better option than having the class read it in silence. Reading aloud is an integral part of the teacher's repertoire in both primary and secondary schools, and is an especially valuable tool for teaching stories in classes where there is significant variation in pupils' reading age. Even children who are not yet able to read can enjoy the twists and turns of a good story – and do so long before they start formal schooling – through bedtime stories, picture books, computer games, videos and television – and having a story read aloud in class gives them a chance to contribute to discussion of plot and character on equal terms with those in the class who are already able to read.

An expressive reading from a book makes a significant difference to the listener, as Gamble and Yates (2002: 122) argue:

> Reading aloud is a dramatic event; the adult reader's own interpretation and understanding allow him or her to emphasize the clues and signs required to fill in the gaps in the text using

---

[6] For a detailed description of preparing and telling a story see Steve Woodward's account of teaching Odysseus and the Lotus-Eaters in Woodward 1980: 37–51. For discussion of how to teach history through story see Fines and Nichols 1997: 188–92.

paralinguistic and prosodic cues in the reading performance and the listener can draw on those to help understand the narrative.

Using variations in pace, tone and volume, a good reader can make texts well beyond a pupil's own reading range accessible and enjoyable. This skill is particularly important when teachers are trying to engage pupils with 'texts they might not choose for themselves: stories with unfamiliar contexts, denser argumentative prose, newspaper articles or older, less familiar forms of poetry and narrative' (Margaret Meek, preface to Barrs and Cork 2001: 13) – a text such as the *Iliad*, in fact, as we shall see later. The importance of expressive reading was highlighted in a piece of research conducted by Barrs and Cork in five primary schools in outer London. They examined how pupils' written work developed through engagement with challenging literature, most of which teachers introduced to their pupils through a class reading:

> All read aloud in their most expressive voices, to bring the text alive and engage their children in a reading 'performance' ... This social act of bringing the text alive and lifting it off the page, with the pupils, at first, as listeners, meant that the language and the 'voice' of the author or poet was strongly present in the classroom. It provided an important background for children's own reading of the text, whenever they reread it individually. It seemed likely that this expressive reading would echo in the children's memories, helping them to internalise some of the language of the text. Certainly this seemed to be the case with some children, whose writing showed strong influences of texts that they had heard, but not yet read independently.

> (Barrs and Cork 2001: 72–3)

It is not only that reading aloud is an inclusive activity which provides equal access to stories by removing the barrier of the printed word. By bringing the text to life and lifting it off the page with a reading performance, the teacher helps children absorb the language of the story and work it into their own writing; and at the same time, by bringing the author into the classroom, the teacher makes the story more memorable. This is particularly the case with traditional tales because they 'contain strong literary devices, the tunes, patterns and rhythms that make the language and structures of the stories memorable' (Nicholson 2006: 12). I saw this for myself in numerous interviews with children who had listened to *War with Troy*: many children were able to remember specific vocabulary and whole phrases two or three months after hearing the story, helped by the frequent repetition of the epithets and formulaic phrases used by the storytellers.

There are strong reasons for encouraging teachers to overcome their reservations and try storytelling. Telling rather than reading a story helps create an intimacy between teacher and pupils:

> I have always told masses of stories ... because I have found that when you have got a whole group of children sitting on a carpet, particularly ones that you don't know, if you tell and have eye contact, they are just drawn into the story ... If you have no book ... the children and you develop a relationship much, much quicker. I always tell a lot of stories when I get a new class and it works.
>
> (Primary school teacher quoted in Bage (2000: 40))

Maintaining unbroken eye contact with pupils enables the teacher to monitor their response to the story and adjust the telling accordingly. Furthermore, as a storyteller the teacher can establish a dialogue with the class, interspersing the narrative with questions, drawing the class into the story through discussion of plot and character and through speculation about what might happen next – in short, providing precisely the sort of fast-paced, interactive whole-class teaching advocated by the National Literacy Strategy. There is one other option, to work with a recording of the story, an approach examined in the next chapter.

References

Bage, G. (2000). 'Developing teaching as storytelling', in Cliff Hodges, G., Drummond, M. J. and Styles, M. (eds.), *Tales, Tellers and Texts*, pp. 36–45. London: Continuum International Publishing Group

Barrs, M. and Cork, V. (2001). *The Reader in the Writer*. London: Centre for Language in Primary Education

Cook, E. (1969). *The Ordinary and the Fabulous: An Introduction to Myths, Legends and Fairy Tales for Teachers and Storytellers*. London: Cambridge University Press

DES (1977). *Classics in Comprehensive Schools*. London: HMSO

DES (1988). *Classics from 5 to 16, Curriculum Matters 12*. London: HMSO

DfES (2002). *The National Literacy Strategy: Towards the National Curriculum for English*. London: DfES

Fines, J. and Nichols, J. (1997). *Teaching Primary History*. Oxford: Heinemann

Finley, M. I. (1964). 'Crisis in the classics', in Plumb, J. H. (ed.), *Crisis in the Humanities*, pp. 11–23. Harmondsworth: Penguin

Forrest, M. (1996). *Modernising the Classics: A Study in Curriculum Development*. Exeter: Exeter University Press

Gamble, N. and Yates, S. (2002). *Exploring Children's Literature*. London: Paul Chapman

Grove, N. (2005). *Ways into Literature: Stories, Plays and Poems for Pupils with SEN*. London: David Fulton Publishers

Grove, N. and Park, K. (1996). *Odyssey Now*. London: Jessica Kingsley Publishers

Nicholson, D. (2006). 'Putting literature at the heart of the literacy curriculum', *Literacy* 40(1), pp. 11–21

Rieu, E. V. (1937). *The Story of Odysseus*. London: Thomas Nelson and Sons

Schools Council (1967). *Humanities for the Young School Leaver: An Approach through Classics*. London: HMSO

Sharwood Smith, J. E. (1977). *On Teaching Classics*. London: Routledge and Kegan Paul

Steiner, G. (ed.) (1996). *Homer in English*. London: Penguin Books

Vernant, J.-P. (translated by Asher, L.) (2001). *The Universe, the Gods and Mortals*. London: Profile Books

Woodward, S. (1980). 'Myths and drama in the class-room with 11–13-year-olds', *Hesperiam* 3, pp. 37–51

Modern retellings of classical stories and related literature

Atwood, M. (2005). *The Penelopiad*. Edinburgh: Canongate Books

Curtis, R. and Robinson, T. (1988). *Odysseus: The Greatest Hero of Them All*. London: Knight

Garfield, L. and Blishen, E. (1970). *The God beneath the Sea*. London: Longman

Garfield, L. and Blishen, E. (1973). *The Golden Shadow*. London: Longman

Geras, A. (2000). *Troy*. London: Scholastic Press

Geras, A. (2005). *Ithaka*. London: Scholastic Press

Harris, R. (2003). *Pompeii*. London: Hutchinson

Harris, R. (2006). *Imperium*. London: Hutchinson

Hughes, T. (1997). *Tales from Ovid*. London: Faber and Faber

Kinglake, A. W. (1982). *Eothen*. London: Century Publishing Company

Lancelyn Green, R. (1958). *The Tale of Troy*. Harmondsworth: Puffin Books

Lang, A. (1978). *Tales of Troy and Greece*. London: Faber and Faber

Redmond, D. and Kingsland, R. (1993). *The Comic Strip Odyssey*. London: Puffin Books

Serraillier, I. (1962). *The Way of Danger*. Oxford: Oxford University Press

Serraillier, I. (1963). *The Clashing Rocks*. Oxford: Oxford University Press

Shanower, E. (2001). *A Thousand Ships*. San Diego: Hungry Tiger Press

Shanower, E. (2004). *Sacrifice*. San Diego: Hungry Tiger Press

Sherrill, S. (2003). *The Minotaur Takes a Cigarette Break*. Edinburgh: Canongate Books

Sutcliff, R. (1993). *Black Ships before Troy*. London: Frances Lincoln

Sutcliff, R. (1995). *The Wanderings of Odysseus*. London: Frances Lincoln

Walcott, D. (1990). *Omeros*. London: Faber and Faber

Williams, M. (1998). *'The Iliad' and 'The Odyssey'*. London: Walker Books

4 | The Iliad Project: the development of *War with Troy*

My first experience of teaching the Trojan War was as part of a combined humanities course, based on the story-centred approach discussed in the previous chapter. I was teaching in an inner London school, which was in the process of transition from grammar school to comprehensive, and the Year 7[1] humanities course had been introduced as part of a major revision of the curriculum to help cater for the much wider ability span of the new intake. It brought together classics, history, geography and religious education, with a teacher from each discipline on the team whenever the staffing allowed it. The main classical element of the course was a module on the Trojan War (including Agamemnon's return to Mycenae) and links between myth and history (focusing on Mycenae and the story of Schliemann), which drew heavily on the CSCP Greek World Foundation Course folder, *Troy and the Early Greeks* (CSCP 1972). Partly, no doubt, because I was teaching my own specialism (I could never get so excited by shadufs), this was the humanities module that I most enjoyed teaching and the module which brought out the best work from pupils.

Memories of these classes and the clear evidence from the GRIPS project that myths and legends were well received by teachers and pupils in primary schools were important factors behind the setting up of the Iliad Project in 2000. The decision to set up a project was also motivated by a desire to revisit work done for CSCP by Martin Forrest in the late 1960s and early 1970s. In spite of the initial success of the Greek World Foundation Course, by the 1980s it was proving difficult to sustain story-based classical studies courses in the early years of secondary schools. This may have been partly because of shortcomings with the materials themselves: as early as 1971, Nicholas Whines (1971) argued that the CSCP folders were problematic because their effective use was too dependent on the

---

[1] i.e. children aged eleven to twelve.

organisational skills of the teacher, trying to implement an individual enquiry method in the still unfamiliar context of the mixed ability classroom. But there were other issues outside the control of CSCP or the wider classics community. With growing pressures on the timetable in the early years of secondary school, many classicists found their lesson allocation in Year 7 reduced or cut entirely, and combined humanities courses, which might have provided sufficient time to teach at least one module on Greek mythology, fell out of favour.

Initial funding for the Iliad Project came from CSCP itself, but it was supported later by the Society for the Promotion of Hellenic Studies, who funded a research conference and the purchase of materials for pilot schools, and by the University of Cambridge Aspiration Fund, who gave a substantial grant. The project was jointly led by the author and Grant Bage, a historian with wide experience of primary schools as a teacher and LEA adviser, and involved close collaboration with two professional storytellers, Hugh Lupton and Daniel Morden.

The aims of the Iliad Project were:

- to provide a modern oral, print and digital retelling of the *Iliad* for use in primary schools, capable of adaptation for other settings;

- to create a range of additional learning resources to support Year 5 pupils' learning about the Homeric world and the development of literacy through study of the *Iliad*;

- to create support materials for primary schools teachers, making explicit links between the teaching of literacy and study of the *Iliad*;

- to set up a website giving access to learning resources and other support materials for teachers;

- to trial and evaluate the above across a range of primary schools.

In many ways these aims were very similar to those of Martin Forrest in 1967 when he began development of the Greek World Foundation Course, and underlying the Iliad Project was the same belief in the story-centred approach. There were, however, two significant differences: the target audience was the last two years of primary school rather than the early years of secondary school; and the main emphasis was on the creation of a literary version of the story itself rather than on resources to support and encourage story-based activities. This shift was prompted partly by the wish to fill a perceived gap in the market: no existing version of the story, and particularly no oral retelling, seemed to achieve the right balance of accessibility and authenticity for a young audience.[2] But it was prompted mainly by the practical realities of the curriculum, as discussed in chapter 2: it was felt that because Key Stage 2 was the only phase when classics was part of the compulsory curriculum and because primary schools had been devoting so much time to literacy since the introduction of the literacy hour, few schools were likely to set aside the minimum of twelve hours needed to teach a unit on the Trojan War unless the Iliad Project developed materials with clear links to literacy. Furthermore, there was an obvious overlap between literacy and Homer in the area of speaking and listening, which had been identified as receiving less attention and being less well taught than reading and writing: an oral retelling of a story which was itself the product of an oral tradition had the potential to provide a clear framework for developing pupils' speaking and listening skills.[3] One teacher taking part in the Iliad Project was clear about the importance of this:

> The gain for the children from *War with Troy*, I think, was that it was purely speaking and listening, and it was something in this particular area we were concerned about: that the children weren't confident speakers and we were always moaning that they weren't listening. So all of the other English areas that we have, all of the units of work, basically are geared towards a written outcome and it gave an opportunity to add that dimension to our literacy, that we could just do something that was actually going to enhance the children's speaking and listening.
>
> (School B)[4]

It should be noted that not only classicists but historians, too, are aware that they need to develop explicit links between history and the core curriculum. At an Ofsted conference in 2005, when the main topic was the revision of the history curriculum, Paul Armitage HMI, a subject adviser for history, suggested that the new curriculum should be one that 'recognises the wider needs of pupils and students (for example, literacy, numeracy and personal development) and demonstrates how history supports these other needs' (Ofsted 2005: 2). There has also been a familiar ring to the response from historians to the potential marginalisation of their subject: concerns have been expressed

---

[2] At the one end of the spectrum is Tony Robinson and Richard Curtis's *Odysseus: The Greatest Hero of Them All*, at the other Anton Lesser's reading of Chapman's *Iliad*.
[3] Government concerns culminated in the publication by the DfES of *Speaking, Listening, Learning: Working with Children in Key Stages 1 and 2* in November 2003 as part of the Primary National Strategy. Coincidentally it was published on the day the CD set of *War with Troy* was launched at the British Museum.
[4] School B refers to one of the Iliad Project pilot schools in Barking and Dagenham local authority. For a description of the school, see page 61. In this and subsequent quotations from transcripts, every attempt has been made to report the speaker's words verbatim, unless the sense is lost without editing.

recently that 'history in many primary schools has become or is in danger of becoming a branch of English comprehension especially in Years 2 and 6', i.e. in the run-up to Key Stage 1 and Key Stage 2 SATs.[5]

The creation of *War with Troy*

Although all those involved with the Iliad Project shared the conviction that the *Iliad* was a text that could and should be offered to all pupils in the upper years of primary school, they were also aware of the challenges it presented. For the storytellers there were three main issues. Firstly, how could they reduce the story to a maximum of twelve episodes while not only retaining the sweep and thrust of the original but also providing some context at the beginning and closure at the end of their telling? Secondly, how could they tell the story in simple enough terms to make it accessible to the full ability range while retaining something of the poetry of Homer's language? Thirdly, how should they approach scenes involving sex or violence, which, if described too graphically, might upset or offend pupils, parents and possibly teachers? Having previously created a two-hour version of the *Odyssey*, which they had performed for a number of years, the storytellers understood the challenge of condensing Homer for public performance. But even though they had developed a strong feel for Homer through their work on the *Odyssey*, it took two years to reach a point where they were ready to 'freeze' their oral retelling of the *Iliad* on CD. This was partly because of the complexity of the narrative and the large number of characters (gods and mortals) in the *Iliad*, and partly because of the lengthy process of repeated testing and revision to ensure that the final version met the needs of primary-age children.

Reducing the story to manageable episodes was the storytellers' first task. Ignoring Elizabeth Cook's characteristically assertive comment that 'the legend of the Trojan War is not episodic ... [and] does not fall easily into a series of self-contained lessons' (Cook 1969: 22), Lupton and Morden began by working independently on identifying key scenes, the main building blocks of the narrative, before meeting to compare notes and map out an agreed skeleton of the story (literally – they drew a map of Troy and surrounding land to develop a shared picture of the terrain in their minds) in the form of a storyboard. Having agreed the outline of the story, they again worked independently on the narrative before meeting again to weave it into a unified whole. The whole process, as Hugh Lupton described, was

---

[5] Dr Tim Lomas, Principal School Improvement Adviser for CfBT Lincolnshire School Improvement Service, reported this concern in a newsletter to Lincolnshire primary schools, June 2006.

highly visual: 'when I'm learning a story, I'm learning pictures first and foremost – a sequence of pictures, one following the other. And then the words wind themselves around the pictures and that's certainly how I remember. I haven't got a very good memory for other things but I can remember stories.'[6] It should be stressed that at no point did they commit the story to writing: *War with Troy* was conceived as a spoken not a written text, as a story to be heard not read.

One can see from the description of the storytellers' working methods that *War with Troy* was never meant as a translation of the *Iliad*. As already implied, it goes well beyond the tight time frame of Homer's story – which covers only seven weeks of the last year of the war – and like most adaptations of the *Iliad* for children (for example, Rosemary Sutcliff's *Black Ships before Troy*), it begins with the marriage of Peleus and Thetis and ends with the fall of Troy. Of the twelve episodes of *War with Troy*, the first four set the scene for the 'real' *Iliad* episodes, and the last two describe events after the end of the *Iliad* (the death of Achilles in episode 11 and the fall of Troy in episode 12). The intervening six episodes cover main scenes from the *Iliad*: the argument between Agamemnon and Achilles, Achilles' refusal to fight, Patroclus' intervention after the burning of the Greek ships, the death of Patroclus, the death of Hector, Priam's visit to Achilles, and the burial of Hector.

The duel between Paris and Menelaus is also included but transposed to come before rather than after the argument between Agamemnon and Achilles. This is one of a number of examples of the storytellers making changes to the Homeric original in order to create a narrative that would work with their young audience. Another example is the inclusion of the story of Cygnus' duel with Achilles taken from Ovid's *Metamorphoses* Book XII, which was incorporated in the account of the arrival of the Greek army at Troy to help establish in children's minds, through the vivid description of Achilles' mutilation of Cygnus, the savage ferocity of the central character. The storytellers also included one significant invention of their own, a ring, 'carved in the shape of a curling arrow whose sharp point touches its feathered tail', given to Thetis by Aphrodite on her wedding day, passed on by Thetis to Achilles, who in turn gave it to Patroclus and retrieved it after his death, before giving it finally to Polyxena. Classicists may not be comfortable with this sort of intervention, but for both the tellers and their young audience the ring is an important narrative device that helps them keep track of the changing fortunes of Achilles and those closest to him.

In terms of the language of *War with Troy*, aspects of Homer's

---

[6] Interview, *War with Troy* CD 3

poems, such as repeated epithets and extended similes, spring naturally from the highly visual approach adopted by the storytellers, helping them remember the story and making the story memorable for the listener. Epithets are used particularly for the gods, for example owl-eyed Athene, great father Zeus, Poseidon king of the tumbling foam; and similes are kept wherever possible, though simplified for a young audience. So, for example, when Patroclus goes out to face Trojans in Achilles' armour he is accompanied by the Myrmidons, who are compared to a mass of swarming wasps. In Lattimore's translation the description is as follows:

> Now they who were armed in the company of great-hearted Patroklos went onward, until in high confidence they charged on the Trojans. The Myrmidons came streaming out like wasps at the wayside when little boys have got into the habit of making them angry by always teasing them as they live in their house by the roadside; silly boys, they do something that hurts many people; and if some man who travels on the road happens to pass them and stirs them unintentionally, they in heart of fury come swarming out each one from his place to fight for their children. In heart and fury like these the Myrmidons streaming came out from their ships, with a tireless clamour arising ...
>
> (*Iliad* XVI, 259–67, trans. Lattimore (1951))

In *War with Troy* the description is much shorter, but the central image remains:

> Patroclus, dressed in Achilles' armour – Patroclus, dressed as Achilles – rode out against the Trojans then. Death rode a chariot that day and the Myrmidons fastened on the Trojans, as when a little boy hears a strange sound from within a dead, hollow tree and picks up a stick and pushes the stick into the shadows, and the wasps who have nested inside come pouring out – a seething, black cloud of frenzied rage.

The storytellers tested out extracts from their first version on live audiences in three Cambridgeshire primary schools in spring 2001. Their main concern at this stage was to see how long it took to tell episodes and to gauge whether they had pitched the language of their retelling at an appropriate level. They quickly realised that their initial version of the story was too long and needed simplifying in parts; but as far as the general level of the language of the story was concerned, while there were problems with one or two specific words – for instance, pupils had difficulty with 'oxide' (ox-eyed) Hera – most children had little difficulty understanding individual scenes even when they included some unfamiliar vocabulary. Appropriate amendments were incorporated into a second, shorter, version of *War with Troy*, which was recorded on to CD for further testing in January to March 2002. This was a crucial phase in the piloting of *War with Troy* because at this point not only the revised story but also the transmission of the story by CD was under scrutiny. It was hardly surprising that live performances of extracts from *War with Troy*, followed by drama workshops, had enthralled children. It was much less predictable how they would respond to listening to the story on CD two or three times a week as part of the literacy hour, with their classroom teacher at the front of the class rather than two unfamiliar storytellers.

This phase of the pilot was conducted in five schools, none of which had been involved in the earlier trialling involving live performances. Three of the schools were in an Education Action Zone (set up in the late 1990s to improve standards through collaboration between schools) in Thetford and two in Barking and Dagenham local authority in east London. The evaluation of *War with Troy* was based on classroom observation, interviews (with pupils and teachers) and a questionnaire. No new issues emerged concerning the structure and length of the story, but some concerns were expressed about the content of one or two scenes, such as Zeus' seduction by Hera, and Paris and Helen's leisurely voyage from Sparta to Troy, 'leaving their imprint in the sand on every island across the Aegean'. In one case the teacher admitted that difficulties arose as much from nervousness about how the children might react rather than from the children's actual responses; in another case, the teacher had used the story with Year 4 children, for whom the battle scenes were rather too graphic. But the following response summed up the general view about the potentially problematic scenes:

> There's no bits that I would want changed. When I read the transcripts or listened to the CD, I thought 'Oh, I'll have to watch out for this bit, you know because there'll be some sniggers and the first bit, you know, where they stop off at every island – Paris and Helen stop off at every island – I thought 'Oh dear, I hope they don't start asking me questions about that', but they didn't actually.
>
> (School C)

And with regard specifically to the battle scenes, the same teacher said:

> [I'm not worried about the graphic descriptions] because they're in context. I think it is part of the story; it's about a war, isn't it? I mean you can't have a war without killings and blood and gore and all the rest of it. So I think it's not sensationalised – it's told as it is – and I think it's good.
>
> (School C)

As a result, while one or two amendments were made, the contentious scenes remained in the story.

Encouragingly, both teachers and pupils liked having the story on CD. One teacher commented that

> It's having that extra voice in the room or voices that you can actually relate to. You can talk to the children about the storytellers and it is, it's like having another person in the room with you because the children do get tired of your voice all the time. And it is nice to listen to something that is totally different. It is a new experience for them to have a story told in that way.
>
> (Teacher, School B)

Pupils' enjoyment of the CDs was evident in their responses to the pupil questionnaire. When asked how much they enjoyed reading stories in books, responses from the 236 returns were as follows:

Very much	Quite a lot	Not much	Not at all	No response
94	81	38	15	8

When, on the other hand, they were asked how much they enjoyed listening to *War with Troy*, they responded as follows:

Very much	Quite a lot	Not much	Not at all	No response
159	39	19	5	14

It may not be surprising that pupils much preferred *listening* to *reading*, but it is instructive that of the 38 pupils who said that they did not much like reading stories and the 15 who said they did not like reading stories at all 28 said that they enjoyed listening to *War with Troy* very much and a further 13 answered 'quite a lot'. Although that leaves 12 pupils who derived little pleasure from listening to the story, the fact that more than three quarters of the reluctant readers enjoyed listening quite a lot or very much suggested that a CD recording of a story, while not the same as hearing the story told live, was still an effective medium for engaging and stimulating a wide range of pupils.

One practical issue emerged from the second phase of the pilot: the need to break down the twelve episodes into shorter scenes. While experienced teachers quickly became adept at finding suitable points at which to pause, for instance to clarify or discuss points in the story, it was clear that if the episodes were broken down into shorter units it would provide additional support for inexperienced teachers and make navigation of the CDs considerably easier.

In April 2002, at the end of the second phase of testing, a two-day closed conference was held in Cambridge to discuss possible changes to the 'text' of *War with Troy* and find out how it had been used in the classroom. This conference brought together nine teachers from the pilot schools, three people involved with the project at an LA level, and three of the Iliad Project team. As well as sharing classroom experiences and making initial attempts to identify learning gains made by pupils from listening to *War with Troy*, those attending the conference discussed a possible teacher's guide to accompany the CDs. It was recognised that without substantial support for the CDs in terms of background information and suggested teaching activities, it would be difficult to persuade primary school teachers with little or no knowledge of Greek mythology to teach the Trojan war, even if there were clear evidence from the classroom that the story was popular with pupils; they would need convincing that literacy skills could be addressed through the story. From the ideas pooled at the conference a framework for episode-by-episode notes was developed, and the notes themselves were subsequently written by a teacher from one of the pilot schools as part of the published *War with Troy Teacher's Guide*. The notes include suggestions for activities before and after listening to an episode linked wherever appropriate to the relevant teaching and learning objectives set out in the National Literacy Strategy (DfEE 1998), the guidelines for speaking and listening (DfES/QCA 2003), and the guidelines for personal, social and health education and citizenship (DfEE/QCA 1999). The guide also includes a summary of each episode, a full transcript and fifteen photocopiable illustrations, most of which are line drawings based on decorations from Greek pottery, as in figure 2 below.

Figure 2 *'Peleus and Thetis', from the* War with Troy Teacher's Guide; *reproduced with permission of the Cambridge School Classics Project*

References

Cook, E. (1969). *The Ordinary and the Fabulous: An Introduction to Myths, Legends and Fairy Tales for Teachers and Storytellers*. London: Cambridge University Press

CSCP (1972). *Troy and the Early Greeks*. Cambridge: Cambridge University Press

DfEE (1998). *The National Literacy Strategy: A Framework for Teaching*. London: DfEE

DfEE/QCA (1999). *The National Curriculum for England: Non-Statutory Frameworks for Personal, Social and Health Education and Citizenship at Key Stages 1 & 2*. London: DfEE/QCA

DfES/QCA (2003). *Speaking, Listening, Learning: Working with Children in Key Stages 1 and 2*. London: DfES/QCA

Lattimore, R. (1951). *The Iliad of Homer*. Chicago: Chicago University Press

Ofsted (2005). *Ofsted Subject Conference Report: History* (HMI 2510). London: Ofsted

Whines, N. (1971). 'The CSCP non-linguistic course: a critique', *Didaskalos* 3 (3), pp. 507–19.

5 | Responses to *War with Troy*

The three-CD set of *War with Troy* and accompanying *Teacher's Guide* were published in autumn 2003. Shortly after the storytellers completed the final recording in summer 2002, a further evaluation began, with the aim of assessing the value of *War with Troy* as a resource for teaching literacy for a wide range of pupils.[1] The evaluation was carried out in six schools in Barking and Dagenham local authority (LA), Schools A and B (described in detail below), which had taken part in the initial CD pilot, and four further schools (Schools C to F). Before looking at the findings, it will be helpful to give a little background information about the LA and, since they provided much of the data for the evaluation, the two schools with most experience of using *War with Troy* in the classroom.

The context

Barking and Dagenham LA is part of the Thames Gateway area east of London and is primarily residential, with Ford Motors the main local employer. In 2000 it was rated the sixth most deprived borough in London (and twenty-fourth nationally), and had the lowest number of adults with higher education qualifications in the country.[2] Since then, after a long period of stability, there have been significant changes in the borough, partly because of the borough's largest employer reducing its workforce, and partly because of a steady influx of refugees and asylum seekers. The LA still operates along traditional lines and continues to provide a highly valued advisory service. In 1996, two years before the introduction of the National Literacy Strategy, it pioneered a primary English curriculum based on high-quality texts (including *Sir Gawain and the Loathly Lady* and Alfred Noyes's *The Highwayman* in Year 5, and *The Hobbit*, *The Lady of Shalott*, and *The*

---

[1] This was funded by the University of Cambridge Faculty of Education Research Development Fund.
[2] Data from Ofsted report 2002. Retrieved on 2 May 2006 from http://www.ofsted.gov.uk/reports/servicereports/315.htm.

Lion, the Witch and the Wardrobe in Year 6), and since its introduction Key Stage 2 SATs scores in English have risen across the borough from 36 per cent, reaching level 4+ to 75 per cent in 2005.

School A is a primary school of 325 pupils of whom 25 per cent are from an ethnic minority background. After a critical Ofsted report the school was placed on special measures in 2003. Standards in English at Year 6, however, were deemed satisfactory – pupils' speaking and listening skills were 'broadly as expected', and it was noted that 'a number of pupils are articulate speakers who provide detailed answers, explanations and arguments. They speak clearly, and put their points confidently and concisely. Whilst some are less confident, most are happy to speak in front of other people.' Because Year 5 and 6 pupils are taught in mixed age classes, *War with Troy* has been taught in alternate years. It is taught within the literacy hour over a four-week period, with three speaking and listening sessions and one grammar session a week. The speaking and listening sessions occasionally include a writing task but the primary aim of these sessions is to familiarise the class with the story through listening and discussion.

School B is a junior school with 332 pupils, of whom 13 per cent are from an ethnic minority background. In the most recent inspection report it was described by Ofsted as 'a very effective school' where pupils 'enjoy their lessons, work very hard, and enthusiastically answer questions in class ... They listen to each other's views, work cooperatively, and readily help each other in all aspects of school life ... By the end of Year 6, pupils of all abilities use punctuation, paragraphing and sentence construction effectively to produce interesting pieces of writing. Higher attaining pupils use a wide range of vocabulary to create humour and interest in their writing.' *War with Troy* is generally taught to the whole of Year 5 as a single group (of approximately eighty children) in the school hall, once a week for twelve weeks of the spring term. One Year 5 teacher is designated to lead all twelve sessions; the other teachers sit in on the sessions and help with follow-up activities. As with School A, *War with Troy* is used primarily as a vehicle for developing children's speaking and listening skills and sessions often include drama activities. As a matter of policy very little writing is done during the actual *War with Troy* sessions, though individual classes may undertake writing tasks based on *War with Troy* as part of their regular English lessons.

Although there are significant differences in the way each school incorporated *War with Troy* in the timetable, their approaches to the actual teaching – and those of the other four schools taking part in the evaluation – have been very similar. They all make speaking and listening the main focus of *War with Troy* sessions. Across Barking and Dagenham as a whole, there is strong support for the sort of 'dialogic' approach to teaching advocated by Robin Alexander (2004), i.e. one which promotes pupils' cognitive development through the use of effective speaking and listening strategies; and the teachers in Schools A and B base their teaching on the belief that speaking and listening are skills that can be taught in the same way as any other skill; that, for instance, children who are unused to sitting and listening to someone reading to them or telling them a story can improve their concentration span, or, at a more advanced level, can develop their ability to listen to each other's views and take account of them in their own responses, provided the right conditions for listening are created. To that end the teachers explain the demands of listening in the same way that they would explain the demands of a writing activity, require pupils to put away all unnecessary distractions such as pencils and rulers, and ensure that outside interruptions are kept to a minimum, thereby according status to listening as an activity and heightening the class's expectations and excitement. Pupils are expected to listen to each other with the same respect they give their teacher, no matter how wrong-headed they think the other person's views; and all pupils, irrespective of attainment level, are given the chance, and indeed expected, to express opinions publicly. The corresponding speaking skills are also addressed: pupils are encouraged to speak in a loud, clear voice so that they can be heard by everyone (even in a room containing eighty people); to speak in full sentences and give extended responses to questions; and to apply the public speaking techniques they have learnt through listening to the storytellers (for example variations in volume and pace) in their own classroom presentations.

Findings from the classroom[3]

The most striking feature of lessons and interviews was the evident enthusiasm of pupils for *War with Troy* and the wish to share their enjoyment with others.

> They don't see it as a chore at all, they don't see it as work...
>
> (Teacher, School C)

> The best thing about the *Iliad* is that from the beginning there is pure excitement.
>
> (Year 6 boy, School A)[4]

---

[3] Most of the evidence for the evaluation of *War with Troy* comes from lesson observations and interviews with teachers (mostly individual but also including one extended discussion with five teachers) and with small groups of children. All interviews (and some of the lessons) were video-taped and then transcribed; and as far as possible comments have been left unedited to enable the reader to hear the voice of the contributor, but names of teachers have been changed.

Every Friday I used to walk home telling my mum all about it, it was so fun.

(Year 5 girl, School B)

We had a World Book Day event, you know, six months later ... [and] we thought that they would pick *Harry Potter*, that's what we guessed they'd pick. There was no shifting them, it had to be the *Iliad*.

(Teacher, School A)

They took real pleasure in discussing issues raised by an episode, speculating what might happen next and why, competing to remember minute details from past episodes, and talking about their favourite character or scene. Classes in School A were desperate to have the *Iliad* as their form book and dress up as characters from the Trojan war on World Book Day; the teacher in School B was overwhelmed with volunteers to stay after school and work on a dance production of *War with Troy*. In part the positive attitude of the pupils reflected that of their teachers, for whom teaching *War with Troy* provided welcome relief from the tight constraints of the literacy hour and the National Curriculum more generally:

> Why it was so successful is that you could interpret it in your own way, you could, you know, you could actually do whichever activities you wanted. Some of those activities could come from the children too, if they wanted to, you know, to look at a particular part of it, you could do that. So it wasn't prescriptive.
>
> (Teacher, School D)

> I think it's the freedom to discuss and the idea that they've got a chance to speak and you can then, the next session, or whenever, you can think, 'Mmm, that would be a good thing, let's work with that, we can take that further.' It's not, sort of, Day 1, Week 1 – this is my target, this is what I've got to do. I felt freer with it somehow and therefore I was able to make it more child-centred.
>
> (Teacher, School B)

> As the teacher, you felt that you were enabling your class to understand this story more than with some of the books that we do where ... you do feel under pressure to get through the unit and produce all the work because someone's going to monitor it and check if you've done all the tasks.
>
> (Teacher, School A)

---

[4] In Schools A and B teachers and pupils tended to call *War with Troy* the *Iliad* because no agreement had been reached on the name when the CDs were first tested.

The fact that the teachers enjoyed teaching *War with Troy* because they saw it as a break from the objectives-led, SATs-driven curriculum tells us more, perhaps, about their attitude to the National Curriculum than to Greek myths and legends. But it was a significant factor in the success of *War with Troy*: the enjoyment teachers gained from being able to exercise their professional judgement – in deciding, for instance, how to approach each episode and what sort of follow-up work to set their pupils – was transmitted to the pupils themselves, and they responded with corresponding enthusiasm.

Access and inclusion

But what gave the teachers most pleasure and convinced them of the value of *War with Troy* as a classroom resource was the extent to which it proved accessible to children of widely differing aptitudes and attainment. For low-attaining pupils and reluctant readers the fact that it was an oral rather than a written resource was of fundamental importance:

> The great thing about the actual CD, is that they do not have to worry at all about whether or not they can read it ... It's better when everybody can access it. If you're reading round a class, you've obviously got a wide range of ability in the class and you may be all right for some children, but then when you get the ones that struggle with reading, you lose the plot, don't you? You lose the excitement of the story.
>
> (Teacher, School D)

> Some of my children who don't normally speak up in class are really enthusiastic and joining in and giving their opinions and things ... And I think because the story is something that they are obviously enjoying, that they are prepared to listen, when at other times they may have found it more difficult to listen or take in when they're reading something.
>
> (Teacher 1, School E)

> It's [accessible to] all children from the highest to the lowest attainer: they can each enter the story and become involved in it, which in other lessons they may not, because they are text-bound ... If you're a child that's actually struggled for five years, it's quite disheartening and then all of a sudden you've got this lesson where actually you can join in and can shine.
>
> (Teacher, School B)

As this last comment indicates, it was not merely that lower attainers could understand the work. They could take part in the lesson:

I think the lower attaining pupils tend to gain more because they feel, they don't see themselves as being apart from the rest of the class, which they quite often do. ... They'll read *Sir Gawain* and *The Lady of Shalott* and *The Highwayman* and they will actually understand it, but they can't prove to us that they've understood it because they might have limited writing skills, whereas in this they can actually talk about the story and they talk about it in the same way as maybe somebody who's a brilliant writer ... they can actually take part in the class discussion and give valuable contributions to the lesson in a way that they can't do at any other time.

(Teacher, School C)

I think it gives the children confidence to write because they haven't had to struggle to read and they feel there's something they actually want to write. You know, they've shared something. They've suddenly realised that they are on a level footing with everybody else, that actually what they said was as valuable and they respond to the way, I suppose, that you've responded to their discussion.

(Teacher, School B)

The fact that lower attaining pupils were able to take part in class discussion in the same way as everyone else and no longer felt 'apart from the rest of the class', and could demonstrate that they understood the work through their contribution to discussion enhanced both their self-esteem and their standing with other pupils. Furthermore, this improvement was matched by a shift in the teacher's assessment of their capabilities:

Quite often you realise that you've spent most of the year underestimating a lot of these children and what they can actually do and what they have actually understood, because you're so used to marking their work and they're not very good at writing things down. When you listen to them talking about this story, you think, 'There's nothing wrong with your understanding at all.'

(Teacher, School C)

War with Troy was also seen to be inclusive in terms of gender. Literacy is an area of the primary curriculum where there is a marked discrepancy in the performance of boys and girls (although the gap is closing, in the 2005 Key Stage 2 SATs 84 per cent of girls but only 74 per cent of boys reached level 4, the benchmark at age eleven), and an initial reason for developing the *Iliad* for use in primary schools had been the hope that it might engage boys' interest. One teacher noticed a clear improvement in boys' performance:

Certainly I can think of one or two of the boys again in my class who are not the strongest readers, not the most confident readers, who certainly got a heck of a lot out of it. And their concentration was consequently greater ... It was quite interesting in my class that the people who seemed to respond, the children who seemed to respond openly about it, were the boys.

(Teacher 2, School E)

Another teacher noted an increased interest in reading among boys:

It made my boys that were reluctant readers want to read. They actually wanted to go out and get more stories and ... they brought in books that they'd found in the library. They read, funnily enough, much more than they had previously.

(Teacher, School B)

Most teachers, however, thought that the story appealed as much to girls as to boys, even if there was a feeling that the boys tended to like the fighting and the girls the romance. The evidence from classroom observations suggested that the situation was not so clear-cut: many girls said that they liked the blood and gore, and many boys talked without embarrassment about the underlying themes such as love and friendship, loyalty and betrayal. And although many pupils liked to give the impression that they were bloodthirsty, when discussing war and violence away from the classroom in a small group their responses were thoughtful and measured:

INTERVIEWER   What do you come away thinking about what the storytellers want us to think about war?
BOY 1   Well, they try to tell you that it's not fun and it's not cool. It's bloody and gory and there's killing involved and it's not funny.
INTERVIEWER   It's not funny. Well I think that's a fair summary...
BOY 2   It's just pointless really.
INTERVIEWER   Because?
BOY 3   Because, well, people die and you could kind of have a meeting or a bit more civilised way of sorting it out.
INTERVIEWER   Does it tell us anything about the way that wars start?
GIRL 1   It starts over ridiculous things.

(Interview with pupils in School A)

Teachers tended to focus on the ways in which *War with Troy* brought benefits to lower attainers, but higher attainers were also seen to benefit:

The challenge in the story is something that the high attainers really appreciate and really benefit from, and use again and again in their work. So it doesn't leave them out. They rise to that challenge and enjoy that challenge too and, you know, perhaps try to use the more sophisticated vocabulary...

(Teacher, School A)

Observing higher attainers in the classroom, one could see the pleasure they took in playing with the language. In School A, for instance, *War with Troy* lessons often started with a game to reinforce pupils' knowledge of main characters and places. The teacher shuffled a pack of laminated cards,[5] each with the name of a god, person or place on it, and gave out one to each pupil face down. The pupils took one quick look at their card and then had to come up with a clue to their identity for the rest of the class to guess. The challenge was to come up with obscure but legitimate clues based on the story and the winner was the person whose identity it took longest to guess. As the pupils became familiar with the game, clues became more difficult, and on one occasion the class (and teacher) was stumped by the laconic clue, 'I'm very tall'. Asked to provide a little more help, the boy said, 'I'm very tall. My summit reaches to the heavens'; and he was clearly delighted both with puzzlement caused by his initial clue and with his rather poetic description of Mount Olympus.

Engagement and motivation

When the *War with Troy* CDs were initially piloted, some teachers had reservations about teaching the story to their pupils in the literacy hour because they were uncertain how the pupils would respond to such a challenging story and were unsure whether there would be enough for them to talk about after listening to an episode:

Myself and the other two colleagues all thought, 'Yeah, right. OK. Well, we'll give it a go. But this great Greek classical text with our children? I don't think it's going to work and they'd have to listen for 15 minutes in a lesson to a CD. I just can't see that working but we'll give it a go, you know.'

(Teacher, School A)

One of my reservations with [*War with Troy*] actually in the first place was that the episodes are not very long and I thought, 'Well, I've got an hour's literacy slot here, and they were all going to be

---

[5] Secondary school teachers have much to learn about classroom resources from primary school colleagues. Once the game was over the cards could then be put up on the whiteboard as and when names cropped up and grouped as appropriate (e.g. Greeks and Trojans or gods and mortals).

listening for, sort of, ten, twelve minutes – what do I do with the rest of the time?' And they just talked, they just wanted to talk about it, you know. And lots of discussion came out.

(Teacher, School C)

Initial concerns, then, proved unfounded and in fact it was more often a case of having too little rather than too much time to cover an episode. Comments from pupils show that they very much valued and enjoyed the experience of listening to and discussing the story together:

If you were listening to it by yourself you wouldn't enjoy it as much because when there's people around you, you tend to listen a bit more because you know that everybody is enjoying what you're enjoying ... Also if you enjoyed a certain bit, you can actually tell your friends about it because they'd listened and they can talk about their favourite bits.

(Year 5 girl, School B)

You can discuss it more with your friends and with your teachers and everyone in the class so it's easier to understand.

(Year 6 boy, School A)

You can hear what other people say and you can compare it with your own views, and think, 'Yeah, well that's a bit true' and things like that.

(Year 6 girl, School A)

You could all have your different opinions and put them together, and then you might change your mind about something and think, 'Yes, that's like what it is.'

(Year 6 girl, School A)

The extent to which pupils talked together about *War with Troy* was highlighted by the teacher in School A:

I think because it's on the CD and they're all listening to it together, they talk about it themselves a lot more, like when we're lining up for dinner, you know, you can hear snippets of discussion ... they'll try and predict what's going to happen next or say something about a character.

(Teacher, School A)

In School A, the characters became so familiar to the pupils that they invented nicknames for some of them – for instance, Patroclus was known as Pachocolate – which they used when talking about *War with Troy* in the playground. There was evidence of similar involvement with the characters in School B:

> They would write about a character – they formed huge attachments to characters, and it didn't matter, you couldn't dissuade them, they had real empathy. Achilles was the hero, and it didn't matter how vile he was or how awful his deeds, he was their hero and you couldn't sway them. They were quite strong in who they actually decided that they were going to have as their hero or their villain ... I think [for] some of them [it was] the first time that they'd been that engaged in any story.
>
> (Teacher, School B)

We have already seen that listening to *War with Troy* motivated boys in School B to read more. This increased interest in reading was also noted by other teachers:

> [*The Iliad* and *The Odyssey*] used to sit there gathering dust before [*War with Troy*] came along. Nobody ever chose that book, very few children actually chose it. After this it's the most popular book in the box, everybody wants it.
>
> (Teacher, School C)

> [They read] anything on gods and goddesses. Really it's that factual element as well, isn't it? They can go and find out more about Greece and things like that – they were choosing lots of those books and still do.
>
> (Teacher, School A)

It also stimulated pupils to write:

> You see this whole group of children that actually are quite reluctant writers getting bits of paper and coming in with them the next day, with writing that you haven't even asked for.
>
> (Teacher, School B)

> Most of the time there was no written outcome but sometimes the children actually wanted to do something. A couple suggested writing a play ...
>
> (Teacher, School F)

Perhaps the clearest evidence of the way in which *War with Troy* motivated children was provided by pupils in School B: when the Year 5 pupils were asked to do a creative piece of work based on a favourite scene, more than half the children chose not to draw a picture or write a story or poem but to make a model. And, as one can see from figure 3, some children put a great deal of time and thought into their models.

Figure 3 *Model of Priam's visit by a Year 5 pupil*

In the model in figure 3, a Year 5 girl has captured the moment when Achilles (left, with hands covering his face) receives Priam, King of Troy (kneeling before Achilles), for the body of Hector (lying back left, being eaten by a dog), while Priam's daughter, Polyxena, waits on the cart laden with the gold. Though it is not possible to see on the photograph, the pupil has included specific details from the story, for instance the rope round Hector's ankles, a clear reference to Achilles dragging Hector round the walls of Troy behind his chariot. Not only does the pupil show very good knowledge and understanding of the scene, she also demonstrates that she has absorbed something of the storytellers' language by the way she expresses herself on the label for her model: 'Grey haired King Priam pleads with Achilles for the body of his dear son Hector. The stray dogs are eating Hector's body. Achilles realises Priam is grieving for his son, just as he is grieving for his friend Patroclus. Polyxena is waiting with the cart full of gold, which Priam is offering in return for the body of his son.'

Literacy gains

A key factor in the success of *War with Troy* in engaging and motivating a wide range of pupils was the emphasis on speaking and listening rather than reading and writing. Given this emphasis it would have been surprising if pupils' speaking and listening skills had not improved in the period they studied *War with Troy*. At a basic level teachers noted that by the end of *War with Troy* pupils were able to listen to longer sections of the story without any intervention from the teacher. But of more importance was the willingness of even reticent pupils to contribute to discussion, once they became used to the 'new experience' (see below) of being expected to spend a whole lesson speaking and listening rather than reading and writing:

> And I do think that it's about the whole class being expected to answer – it's not just one or two children ... And [speaking and listening] has been taught through this story and they are expected to take part in the lesson as much as possible. Already, as I said, some of my children who don't normally speak up in class are really enthusiastic and joining in and giving their opinions and things. So already I've noticed a change in some of the children in the way they're responding.
>
> (Teacher 2, School E)

> It was a new experience for them and they obviously liked it ... and they've stayed with it. But the responses – it used to be just one or two, the ones that always put up their hands. But gradually the others have got the confidence to speak up and they know that, even if they get something wrong, they're not going to be sort of shouted down and told off, you know, and it gives them the confidence to speak. And I think everybody spoke today. I was trying to make sure that everybody spoke today.
>
> (Teacher, School C)

Confidence in public speaking and tolerance of other people's views were hallmarks of many of the lessons observed, and we saw earlier (see page 68) that pupils not only enjoyed the discussions they had but also learned from them ('You could all have your different opinions and put them together, and then you might change your mind about something and think, "Yes, that's like what it is"'). In one school they addressed the issue of speaking and listening explicitly by asking the children to analyse the storytellers' techniques:

> If you were to ask the children about the storytellers they would be able to point out how exciting they made it sound. They were able to notice how the voices speeded up or slowed down; they looked at how loud or how quietly they spoke. They picked out all the things you want children, when they are presenting something themselves, to think about really. So for speaking and listening, for giving children an opportunity to practise, and as a good model, it was superb.
>
> (Teacher, School B)

There was also evidence that *War with Troy* helped develop pupils' vocabulary. When asked whether pupils had encountered problems with unfamiliar words in *War with Troy*, one teacher commented:

> I've found they can fill in the gaps. For instance, they weren't sure what *invulnerable* was but they were able to work it out from saying the prophecy.[6] I've not found that to be a problem at all actually and they've done really well. I've been very pleased. And they've used those words. Once they've come into contact with them, they've used the words. Without coming into contact with them, they'd never use them.
>
> (Teacher 2, School E)

The important point here is that having worked out the meaning of words from the context pupils were then willing to make active use of those words themselves. Other teachers reported a similar willingness to use words and phrases from *War with Troy*, in the second case a year after hearing the story:

> I think they learn words and phrases from the actual story. I know there was one example last week ... I was asking about Zeus' feelings after something happened and Fernando said, 'He must have been extremely vexed.' That was absolutely brilliant because he'd never come up with anything like that before.
>
> (Teacher, School C)

> In Year 6, a year later, when opportunities arose, they actually stole phrases, words, metaphors from *War with Troy*, and you'd see it appearing in their writing, which was really quite exciting, that they'd held on to it and used it in the right situation.
>
> (Teacher, School B)

Because the emphasis was on speaking and listening, no systematic attempt was made to investigate to what extent studying *War with Troy* enhanced pupils' writing skills. Teachers did, however, use the story as a starting point for a number of different writing tasks – among other things, pupils wrote diaries, letters, newspapers, obituaries, epitaphs and play scripts. Teachers also commented on the number of pupils who brought in pieces of work they had written unprompted, such as a quiz based on the previous week's episode to use as a starter exercise at the beginning of the next episode (cf. the findings of the GRIPS research on page 16). Occasionally, pupils undertook tasks directly relating to the

---

[6] The context was Thetis dipping Achilles in the river Styx to make him invulnerable. She had been told that if her boy grew up and went to war, though he would win great glory, he would die young.

National Literacy Strategy (NLS) objectives:

> We did do some written tasks, because obviously it's difficult for the teacher not to want some written outcomes. So we had newspaper articles about Helen entering Troy for the first time, and looked at the spoken language and how that differed from the written language, so all of the 'and', 'and', 'and' that you hear in the storytellers, whether that would be acceptable when you were writing. So there was quite a lot of discussion about yes, you can *speak* that way, but no, it doesn't look very good when you *write* that way. For metaphor and simile, it was superb. The children could all see that.
>
> (Teacher, School B)

The work described here addresses two specific NLS text-level objectives (DfEE 1998: 46): pupils should be taught to explore similarities and differences between oral and written storytelling (objective 2); and should be taught to understand the differences between literal and figurative language, e.g. through discussing the effects of imagery in poetry and prose (objective 10).

Appreciation of story

> I think every episode left them wondering what was going to happen next, and they really had a sense of satisfaction that everything tied up at the end. They could see for the first time, some of them, the more challenged children shall we say, the ones that find English quite difficult, they were able to really involve themselves in a plot, in a story, and they could really see all of the loose ends being tied up at the end.
>
> (Teacher, School B)

For many lower attaining pupils, listening to *War with Troy* was the first time in school that they had been absorbed by a long story, a story which, all the teachers agreed, was substantially more challenging than any other stories they read in school (except in School E, where a Year 6 class had read *Hamlet*). They learnt for the first time what it felt like to be bitten by the story bug: they were desperate to hear the next episode and hated it when they missed one (in one school I saw children asking if they could stay in at break-time to catch up on a missed episode), and they found the conclusion to the story both satisfying in so far as all the different strands of the story were tied up, and at the same time disappointing because there was nothing more to come.

Some pupils enjoyed the story as much for the way it had been put together as for its content. In the extract below two pupils from School

A compare *The Hobbit*, which they had recently finished reading, and *War with Troy*, which they had listened to fifteen months earlier:

BOY	Yeah, it's basically, the thing I like about the *Iliad* is that it all links, it all links to each other.
RESEARCHER	Isn't that true of *The Hobbit*?
BOY	*The Hobbit* is a journey so it all goes along [*demonstrating with his hand*].
GIRL	It's an adventure. Like, let's say <u>I was *The Hobbit*</u>[7]
BOY	<u>But it all kind of,</u> in the battle it all comes together.
GIRL	Yeah, I think the battle was good but we missed it because we <u>were on</u>...
BOY	<u>Yeah, I</u> missed the battle...
RESEARCHER	So it was all right in *The Hobbit* when the battle took place?
GIRL	Yeah.
BOY	<u>Yeah</u>. What I hated about *The Hobbit* is that the beginning was boring. It only started to get better. But from the beginning the *Iliad* was, um, so excited (*sic*).
GIRL	He was scared, he was scared, he wanted to smoke a pipe all day...
BOY	Yeah, but the best thing about the *Iliad* is that from the beginning there is pure excitement. Like they already started talking about...
GIRL	There's cliffhangers. Yeah, there's <u>cliffhangers</u>
BOY	<u>Yeah</u>, even on the first one there's cliffhangers.
GIRL	They start off the story, they started the story, then they end it, well kind of end, like cliffhangered it, then started a new one...

These two pupils knew what they were looking for in a story: an arresting opening, a well-constructed narrative and 'cliffhangers' at the end of each episode. And what interested them about the battle in *The Hobbit* was not details of the fighting but the fact that 'in the battle it all comes together'; similarly what they liked about the *Iliad* was the fact that 'it all links to each other' and 'there's cliffhangers'.

Remembering the story

One of the striking aspects of the interview with the two pupils above was the extent to which they remembered many parts of *War with Troy* in close detail. Teachers commented on the ability of their pupils to pick up even the minutest details and recall them long after hearing the story:

---

[7] Underlining indicates overlap between the two speakers.

I'm so impressed that they could actually hold on to [the story] for such a long time. Because they obviously had listened, and they could tell you the tiniest detail so that, you know, I might even get mixed up on something and they'd correct me a year later.

(Teacher, School B)

Actually, I'll tell you what did amaze me, how well some of the children listened, in the sense they picked up on things that I had missed. Sometimes when I was saying something had happened, then some would say, 'No, that didn't happen then', and in actual fact when I listened to the tape again, the CD again, in actual fact they were correct. That's how really, really intently they'd listened to pick up really minute details.

(Teacher, School D)

The teachers suggested that the pupils remembered the story so well because they had listened very carefully, but the type and form of the story were perhaps contributing factors also. Nicholson (2006), stressing that traditional tales had played a special part in her research project, notes that:

Folktales contain strong literary devices, the tunes, patterns and rhythms that make the language and structures of the stories memorable, helping readers and writers hold on to them.

(Nicholson 2006: 12)

But it may also be connected with the very visual nature of the storytelling (see Hugh Lupton's description of the way the storytellers work, page 54). The story conjures up a very vivid picture in pupils' minds (that is evident, for instance, in the model on page 70), which is all the more powerful because it is created by the pupils themselves:

When I was talking to the children in my class today who did it a year ago, so current Year 6s, they were talking about the CD of the *Iliad* that we did in school compared with the film of *Troy*, and comparing that and saying what they preferred and what they didn't. And something that they said was, the story was better when they listened to it because there was more atmosphere. In the film they could see what was happening but in the story they could imagine what was happening and that made it much, much more vivid for them. And they've kept that with them more than, more than something that they might have read, more than something that they would have seen.

(Teacher, School A)

The same point was made in slightly different terms by the two pupils who compared the *Iliad* and *The Hobbit*:

RESEARCHER   So you'd like, you'd like to have more stories on tape that you could listen to?

GIRL   Yeah, because you could get the actual thing [*tapping her forehead*] in your head...

BOY   Yeah.

GIRL   ... that would be better.

BOY   It's kind of, like, <u>you have more time to think</u>[8]

RESEARCHER   <u>What do you mean</u> you get the actual thing in your head?

GIRL   The actual image.

BOY   It's kind of like you have more time to think about it.

Summary

The evidence from the evaluation of *War with Troy* suggests that a tightly constructed, episodic story combined with a predominantly oral approach provides a powerful context for improving not only pupils' speaking and listening skills but also their reading and writing skills, or at the very least their *attitude* to reading and writing. Listening to *War with Troy* was an enjoyable experience for a wide range of pupils, which gave the lower achieving and more reticent pupils the confidence to contribute to lessons and encouraged many pupils to pursue their interest in the story outside the classroom. In a speech to mark World Book Day in March 2005, David Bell, Her Majesty's Chief Inspector of Schools, asserted that 'for me, reading is first and foremost about pleasure'. This is the way we want pupils to view not just reading but learning more generally when they leave primary school, and there was unanimous agreement among teachers that pupils' attitude to work, in terms of engagement and motivation, noticeably increased when they were studying *War with Troy*.

These findings support the case put forward by Nicholson for putting literature at the heart of the literacy curriculum, who concludes her article by saying:

> Experience of challenging literature, opened up for them by skilled teachers, has a profound impact on children's growth as writers. Through experiencing these texts in powerful ways, the children in these classrooms were prepared to look closely at the features of style, language, characterisation and plot that contributed to their effectiveness ... What really does seem

---

[8] Underlining indicates overlap between the two speakers.

crucial, after all this preparation and support, is to give proper time each day for children to practise their art and to be writers.

(Nicholson 2006: 20).

While she was looking specifically at the relationship between literature and the development of pupils' writing, the evidence from the Iliad Project suggests that the benefits of literature apply to literacy more widely. But, as she says, the literature must be 'challenging'. Unless children are encountering literature that raises issues that are important to them and ask questions of them, they will not be interested in trying to uncover meaning and will not be provoked into asking questions themselves. As Robert Protherough says,

> one of the marks of the best fiction for children is that it leaves the readers sufficient room to remake the book as they read it, bringing to it their own experiences of life and of other books, giving characters and incidents a concrete form, filling in what is implied rather than stated, speculating and questioning, judging and sympathising. Trivial, undemanding books spell everything out; they leave nothing for the reader to do; stock formula stories eliminate all sense of the unexpected. One of the reasons that we rarely find filmed versions of novels satisfactory is that they eliminate the imaginative opportunity for us to 'construct' and visualize characters and incidents for ourselves.

(Protherough 1983: 28–9)

War with Troy measures up well against Protherough's criteria.

References

Alexander, R. (2004). *Towards Dialogic Teaching: Rethinking Classroom Talk*. Cambridge: Dialogos

DfEE (1998). *The National Literacy Strategy: A Framework for Teaching*. London: DfEE

Nicholson, D. (2006). 'Putting literature at the heart of the literacy curriculum', *Literacy* 40(1), pp. 11–21

Protherough, R. (1983). *Developing Response to Fiction*. Milton Keynes: Open University Press

6 | *War with Troy* in action

'First Blood': an example

Let us look now at the planning and teaching of a lesson in School B in which a Year 5 class listened to episode 4, 'First Blood' (see appendix 2 for a full transcript of the episode). In this episode the Greek fleet arrives at Troy, and in the first clash of the war Achilles finds a way to kill Cygnus, the Trojan warrior whom no weapon could harm. The lesson was held in the school hall (which, as in many primary schools, doubles as the gym and dining area) with the pupils sitting in a line two deep at the front of the hall and the teacher facing them with the CD player at her side. Unusually for School B, the class comprised a single form of twenty-six pupils (rather than the whole year group) because there had been issues concerning their behaviour.

Table 2 *Lesson plan (Year 5, School B)*

Warm-up	Review of previous episode	10 minutes
	• Recap on arrival of Helen and Paris from Sparta (whole-class question and answer)	
	• Who was in the right, the Greeks or the Trojans? (discussion in pairs)	
Activity 1	Preparing for episode 4: imagining the scene	5 minutes
	• What was it like to be a Greek warrior seeing Troy for the first time? (discussion in pairs, with picture stimulus)	
Activity 2	Preparing for episode 4: imagining the scene	10 minutes
	• What was it like to be a Trojan catching sight of the Greek fleet for the first time? (small group freeze-frames, followed by presentations to whole class)	

Activity 3	Episode 4: 'First Blood'	25 minutes
	• Played in 4 sections, interspersed with whole-class question and answer	
Activity 4	Episode 4 in context	10 minutes
	• Who was responsible for the war? (small group discussion, followed by presentations to whole class)	
Wind-down	Preparation for follow-up writing exercise	5 minutes

Perhaps the most immediately noticeable aspect of the lesson plan shown in table 2 is the amount of time, almost half the lesson, devoted to preparing the ground for the new episode. There is a particular reason for doing so in the case of this episode: 'First Blood', as the title suggests, marks the start of the fighting at Troy and it is essential, before hearing the episode, that pupils have clearly in their minds who the main protagonists are (including gods and goddesses) on each side and what the Greeks and Trojans might be feeling as they prepared for their first confrontation on the battlefield. But with any story spread over a number of episodes – and especially if the lessons take place only once a week – every lesson should begin with some form of scene-setting: the better the class understands the context, the more they will be able to follow the story, and the better they follow the story, the more they will enjoy it.

A second feature of the lesson is the use of whole-class teaching as the dominant teaching style. This is in line with the approach recommended by the National Literacy Strategy which, as we have seen, strongly advocates highly interactive and fast-paced whole-class teaching in the literacy hour. (It is in sharp contrast, on the other hand, to prevailing methods in mixed ability classrooms thirty years ago, when whole-class teaching was seen by supporters of child-centred learning as authoritarian and the emphasis instead tended to be on independent and small group work.) By dividing the lesson into short but closely interconnected activities – no activity lasts more than ten minutes (activity 3 is in reality four activities) and there are four breaks, even if only brief ones, from the whole-class format – the lesson has the variety needed to sustain the pupils' engagement and motivation. But, as we shall see, the teacher also achieves this through varying the type of dialogue she has with the class and the range of responses she expects from them.

The lesson began with a brief consideration of the title, when the class was encouraged to speculate about possible reasons for calling the episode 'First Blood'. In quick succession three boys suggested 'It sounds bloodthirsty', 'It sounds like it's got a lot of action in it' and 'Could be lots of blood'; and lots of blood, the third boy suggested, could be caused by war. Having established that 'First Blood' might describe the outbreak of war, the teacher drew on the pupils' recall of the previous episode to remind them of the immediate cause for the war (the 'theft' of Helen) and the response of the Trojans to her arrival in Troy (anger at the news of her arrival, enchantment on seeing her), before sending them off in pairs to decide which side they would choose to be on and why.

By the end of two minutes, when the class reconvened, all the pupils had had the chance to voice their thoughts privately, and many were ready to do so publicly.

Lesson extract 1

TEACHER Right, if someone in a very loud voice can tell me whose side they would be on, that would be really good. [*A number of hands go up.*] But I want not just 'I would be on the Greek side', 'I would be on the Trojan side', I want to know *why*. So that's harder, isn't it? You think you could? Yes? OK, off you go then.

PUPIL 1 I would be on the Trojans, because, um, I believe that you should have a fair share, and that, um, he picked, um, to give the Golden Apple to Aphrodite, and er, she made him fall in love with Helen and now it's his.

TEACHER So Helen is his – no choice about it, she's chosen him? OK, anybody disagree? Anybody disagree?

PUPIL 2 I disagree. I like both of them, but the Greeks are more powerful. They have goddesses of war and gods of war.

TEACHER So you're going to be on the winning side, Pupil 2? [*Laughs.*] Well, that's not a bad thing, is it? I'm going to be on the winning side.

PUPIL 3 I disagree with Pupil 2, because I think the Trojans are the best side to be on.

TEACHER Why?

PUPIL 3 Because when they start, when they wanted to get Helen, they all start, when she came through the door, she, they all loved, they all start, wanted to marry her.

TEACHER And it's really hard when you love something to give it up. They feel that she's theirs.

The teacher prefaces the discussion by clearly conveying her expectations for the presentation and content of their responses: she is looking for 'a very loud voice' – she repeats this during the lesson – and she wants to know the reasons behind their decisions. By acknowledging that the latter may be hard, she is helping to create a supportive atmosphere in which even less confident or less articulate pupils may feel encouraged to share their ideas with the class.

Giving the pupils the opportunity to think through their responses in pairs leads to the pupils putting forward a variety of reasons for supporting one side or the other. These answers require a sensitive response from the teacher: in her response to Pupil 2, for instance, she seeks to acknowledge and respond directly to the individual while at the same time improving his response, by providing the missing link in his argument and putting it in terms accessible to the rest of the class. Pupil 3's response needs particular care: he seems confident enough (he is prepared to disagree openly with Pupil 2), but his faltering attempt to justify his choice suggests that he has difficulty marshalling his thoughts. However, the teacher's carefully worded response ('And it's really hard when you love something to give it up') implicitly endorses the pupil's contribution; and his fellow-pupils listen patiently, allowing him to think through his answer aloud without interruption. This sort of supportive environment will encourage him to continue taking risks in front of the class.

After establishing who the two sides are who are preparing to fight over Helen and rehearsing with the class possible reasons for supporting one side or the other, the teacher sought ways to help them visualise what it would have been like to be there in Troy on the day the Greek fleet appeared. She started by giving out a picture of Troy as viewed across the plain from the sea, a visual reminder of the description of Troy with which episode 3 had closed:

> A broad beach of white sand; behind it a long flat fertile plain, fields, farms, vineyards, shambling cattle. On each side of the plain, a wriggling river. Behind each river, a long ridge leading to a headland overlooking the sea. At the back of this plain, a city wrapped in stone, the walls as tall and broad as any they'd ever seen. Behind the city, a mountain rose into cloud. Those who saw that sight then felt a tingling, a mingling in their guts of excitement and terror.

After briefly considering the Greek perspective and what it might mean to feel a mixture of excitement and terror, the teacher then shifted the focus to the Trojans, talking to the class as if they were there with her on the battlements of Troy alongside the citizens as they looked out across the plain towards the sea.

Lesson extract 2

TEACHER   Can you see the sea, or the flat land leading down to the sea? Well, I want you all to imagine now that you are citizens of Troy. You're all Trojans. You are the people that had the stones in your hand, ready to stone Helen. But what's happened? [*Plenty of hands go up.*] What's happened?

PUPIL 1   When she walked through the door, she, all of them stopped and they all loved her.

TEACHER   You've all fallen in love with her. You don't want her to go back to the Greeks. You want to keep her. Paris, he's your prince. Your king has said, 'We will keep her. We're powerful, we're strong. We're secure in our city. Nobody's going to harm us.' But in the distance, can you see the blue sea? Right in the distance, I want you to imagine that you're standing on those walls. You know that there's going to be a war now. You know that there's going to be a war. And you have heard that the Greeks are going to bring with them a fierce warrior. What's the name of the fierce warrior that you've heard about?

[*A couple of hands go up.*]

PUPIL 2   Achilles.

TEACHER   [*in a hushed voice*] Achilles. In fact, you don't even say his name aloud, you're so frightened of him. It's the stories about how fierce he is, how powerful he is, you've all heard them. And you know that when you see the little specks in the distance on that blue water – have a look at it, right on the horizon there – one of those ships that's coming towards your city, Achilles is on it. And you can see not one ship, not two, but hundreds crammed packed full of Greek warriors, fierce warriors... I want you, in your groups, to think about if you're standing – have a look again at that picture – you're standing on those walls, and you see those ships approaching, I want you to show me in your little groups, I want you to make a picture for me, of what you might be doing and I want your face to show me how you're feeling ... Before you go into your groups, what might you be doing? You've seen that the ships are on the horizon now, you know that war is coming.

PUPIL 3   Some people would be hiding under the...

TEACHER   You might be hiding. Yeah, what else might you be doing?

PUPIL 4   You might be out [indistinct words].

TEACHER	You're all going to be cowardly Trojans, are you? I thought the Trojans were fierce.
PUPIL 5	You can, like, make a signal at the top and tell them to open the doors and fight.
TEACHER	You might, you might be gathering your army together.
PUPIL 6	If I was a Trojan I would just give up.
TEACHER	[*incredulous*] You'd just give up? You're going to just give up?
PUPIL 6	I'd just surrender.
TEACHER	Well then, your group might show that.

The teacher has only limited success in transporting the pupils to the walls of Troy through her dramatic monologue. Pupil 3's response to her first question is factually correct but his use of the third person shows that he is still very much in the school hall rather than on the walls of Troy. The teacher glosses over this, repeating his answer but in the second person, before trying to draw them into the scene by the use of direct speech and vivid description and then turning again to the illustration she had given out earlier. Even so, it is only when Pupil 6 says 'If I was a Trojan I would just give up' that a pupil demonstrates any real degree of empathy with the Trojans. Unfortunately – as the teacher cannot help showing – it is not the response she was hoping for. Her description of the powerful Achilles and his many fierce companions, it seems, has convinced the class that the Trojans are no match for the Greeks! It is always possible with prediction exercises that the class will not predict correctly how the story unfolds; and what matters most in this activity, and in the linked activity where the pupils create a tableau, is not whether they have the right answer but that they make a personal response based on their reading of the situation and can explain, and if necessary justify, their response to others. Hence the teacher agrees (if a little reluctantly!) that Pupil 6's group could show the Trojans surrendering. We should not be surprised that the pupils found it hard to project themselves into the Trojans' position. These were nine- and ten-year-old children for whom there were only very tenuous links between their world and the world of Troy. By the end of *War with Troy*, however, after listening to the storytellers week after week and exploring the story through creative activities such as drama and movement, many will develop a much stronger sense of empathy with the Trojans (or the Greeks).

The preparation and discussion of the tableaux took ten minutes and by now, nearly twenty-five minutes into the lesson, the class was more than ready to listen to 'First Blood'. Gathering the pupils round the CD player at the front of the class, the teacher provided one last pointer to help focus their attention.

Lesson extract 3

TEACHER Come a little bit closer together here so that we're all a little bit more grouped together. Don't make the line so long. We're going to group round. This [*pointing at the CD player*] is what we're listening to so you can group yourself round a little bit. It'll be nicer to be in a group. Right, are we ready to listen? 'Cause you're going to have to listen very, very carefully. 'First Blood' – I can't wait. There is the most amazing description at the beginning and it describes them getting ready, just what you were doing, getting ready for this battle that is going to come. There's a wonderful simile. What's a simile? [*Several hands go up.*]

PUPIL A word what, er, what … like, like if you put, like, it was as sharp as a shark's tooth.

TEACHER Something that helps us – that's a really good example – that helps us to picture something. Who saw the pictures of the tsunami and the hurricanes on the television? [*Several hands go up.*] And did you see how the rivers became huge and swollen and they uprooted trees? Well, if you listen very carefully, and you do have to listen carefully, you will hear that's how Homer described the two armies meeting, like two raging rivers full of uprooted trees, flotsam, all the debris that they pulled with them, describing them smashing and crashing into each other. So I really want you to see if when you are listening you've got that picture in your head. [*Four-second pause*]. And [*dramatically*] the Greeks don't know it – we're Trojans at the moment, aren't we? We're all citizens of Troy – they don't know that we have got a hero of our own. They've got Achilles, and we are frightened of Achilles, but listen to *our* hero, to the way he's described and what's special about him. OK?

Just as we saw the teacher earlier emphasising the importance of speaking with a loud voice, here she emphasises to the class the importance of listening very carefully to the story; and to create the right atmosphere she encourages them to gather round her in a close group. To give a focus to their listening she highlights three descriptions to listen out for: firstly, the Trojans preparing for battle; secondly, the two armies crashing together; and thirdly, the Trojans' secret weapon ('*our* hero' as the teacher puts it, reminding the pupils whose side they are on). She also takes the opportunity to check how well pupils have understood similes, and to drop in the word 'flotsam' which she feels might be unfamiliar. While the comparison between the tsunami and a river is not strictly accurate, the image of rushing water is likely to be firmly fixed in the children's minds from television coverage so that hearing the description should be all the more vivid in their minds:

> And with a crash of bronze against bronze, the Trojans met the Greeks wading ashore, as two rivers in full spate, each one with a flotsam of uprooted trees, might crash into one another. So it was the Trojans met the Greeks.

Twenty-five minutes into the lesson the class began listening to the new episode, and the episode itself, which lasts just under ten minutes, took a further twenty-five minutes to play through, with pauses for discussion and clarification. The teacher paused first after Cygnus' initial success on the battlefield ('leaving a wake of dead behind himself as he fought'); then, after Achilles' horse spoke to him ('No man could ever harm you. But a god could'); and finally, after the killing of Cygnus ('Cygnus' head was half-torn from his body and every last shudder of life was gone from him'). If we look at the discussion that took place at the third pause, we can see what form the teacher's interventions took.

Lesson extract 4

TEACHER	What did Achilles discover that he could use against Cygnus? Because he tried weapons. What did he use?
PUPIL 1	Armour.
TEACHER	(*Intake of breath*) The boss on the shield. Does anybody know what the boss on a shield is?
PUPIL 2	Is it, the bit where you hold it?
TEACHER	No, but a good guess.
PUPIL 3	Is it the bit what sticks out and it's like a ball, a semi-circle?
TEACHER	Absolutely right. Well done. It's the front of the shield, it's the part in the centre usually, isn't it? And what did he do with it? Ugh, I'm glad I'm not having this before dinner.
PUPIL 4	He punched his nose with it and Achilles left Cygnus' nose smeared over his face.
TEACHER	Ugh. So he's found a way to defeat him and if he's defeated Cygnus he is going to be famous, isn't he? So who's winning now? Who's winning now?
PUPIL 5	Achilles.
TEACHER	Achilles is winning. Which means which side is winning?
PUPIL 6	The Greeks.
TEACHER	The Greeks. We're Trojans though. We're Trojans at the

moment. How are we feeling? You've just watched Cygnus, you've seen what's happened to him. You've seen what Achilles is like.

PUPIL 7   I would feel OK because Cygnus is the goddess of foam's son so the horse said to Achilles that only a goddess could kill you.

TEACHER   Only a god, yes.

PUPIL 7   So the god of foam's son has been killed by him so I reckon the god of foam might kill him back.

TEACHER   Well, well done. Where did you remember the god of foam from?

PUPIL 7   [*whispers*] Zeus' brother. [*aloud*] Zeus' brother.

TEACHER   Right. Right from the beginning of the story, the god of the tumbling foam.

Almost a third of the class are involved in this exchange as the teacher seeks to check on their understanding of the passage and once more explores their feelings as Trojans after watching the death of their hero, Cygnus. Aware of the wide span of ability and attainment, she is not afraid to check apparently simple aspects of the story ('Who's winning now?'); but she also takes time to explore an item of vocabulary ('boss') which might seem relatively unimportant but is the key to understanding how much damage Achilles caused Cygnus. But the most instructive part of this extract is the exchange between the teacher and Pupil 7: the pupil is given time to develop her point of view, supported by the teacher, who is able to identify in the pupil's initial response the seeds of a perceptive response. The pupil has used the information she has gleaned from 'First Blood' – (a) that Cygnus was the son of Poseidon, and (b) that Achilles could be killed only by a god – to conclude that the Trojans would feel 'OK' because there was a good chance that Poseidon would take revenge on Achilles for the death of his son, Cygnus. The pupil for her part shows that she is a good listener, picking up on the teacher's intervention to change Poseidon from goddess to god. (This provides evidence of the value of epithets – Poseidon and foam are clearly strongly linked in the pupil's mind.)

The aim of looking at these interchanges has been to consider how an experienced teacher makes listening to an episode of *War with Troy* an active and inclusive exercise through effective deployment of different types of talk. In extract 1 the teacher uses 'recitation' as a way of warming up the class: she is looking for right answers – even though she has asked them an apparently open question (whose side would you be on, and why?) – to help recreate in the pupils' minds an accurate picture of the story so far as a springboard for speculating what will happen next. In extracts 2 and 3 her style is expository, but dressed up in a dramatic form that provides a bridge for the storytelling to follow. In extract 4, on the other hand, we find something much closer to what Alexander would term 'dialogue', where the pupil is given an extended 'turn' and given a real opportunity to think through a question.

Such 'dialogic' teaching can 'harness the power of talk to engage children, stimulate and extend their thinking, and advance their learning and understanding' (Alexander 2004: 27), but is, according to Alexander, relatively uncommon in England. Drawing on a comparative study of classroom practice in England, France, India, Russia and the United States, Alexander argues that the status, context and uses of talk are strikingly different in many English classrooms from those in other countries where, among other things:

- Oracy[1] is regarded as no less important than literacy.

- There is a strong tradition of oral pedagogy, with sustained oral work in most lessons, and indeed lessons which are oral from start to finish.

- The purpose of classroom talk is seen as mainly cognitive, whereas in England it tends to be seen as primarily social and affective.

- Questions are designed to encourage reasoning and speculation, not just to elicit 'right' answers, and children are given time to think things out, and indeed to think aloud.

- ... Teaching has pace, but without the clock-watching pressure which has come to be associated with the advocacy of 'pacy' teaching by Ofsted and the national strategies.

- The culture of classroom talk is more public and confident. Children talk clearly and loudly. They listen and they expect to be listened to.

- Other aspects of teaching support talk, not least by securing and maintaining children's attention and time on task. These include: classroom layout and pupil organisation; the structure and sequencing of lessons; the handling of time and pace; the context of routines and rules.

- From the way they themselves use language it is clear that teachers believe that they have a responsibility to model talk at its best.

(Alexander 2004: 14–16)

Traditional stories and storytelling (even when encountered through CD rather than live performance) provide a powerful context for

---

[1] According to Alexander, this term was coined by Andrew Wilkinson in *Spoken English* (Birmingham: Birmingham University Press, 1965).

dialogic teaching because they are by nature associated with events and occasions where groups of people come together to listen to, and talk about, things that matter. In the case of the 'First Blood' lesson, from the initial planning of the lesson as a speaking and listening exercise, with a series of linked activities requiring different oral and aural skills, to the organisation of pupil grouping and actual delivery of the lesson, it can be seen to conform to Alexander's model of dialogic teaching which he characterises as:

> *collective*: teachers and children address learning tasks together, whether as a group or as a class;
>
> *reciprocal*: teachers and children listen to each other, share ideas and consider alternative viewpoints;
>
> *supportive*: children articulate their ideas freely, without fear of embarrassment over 'wrong' answers; and they help each other to reach common understandings;
>
> *cumulative*: teachers and children build on their own and each others' ideas and chain them into coherent lines of thinking and enquiry;
>
> *purposeful*: teachers plan and steer classroom talk with specific educational goals in view.
>
> (Alexander 2004: 27)

The lesson can also be seen to provide an example of both education *in* classics and education *through* classics, to use John Sharwood Smith's distinction (Sharwood Smith 1977: 9). In the mind of the teacher it was as important that the pupils developed their understanding of the story of the Trojan War and what it meant to be besieged in Troy, facing an enemy like Achilles, as it was that they developed their speaking and listening skills. The two aims went hand in hand. The success of the lesson (and, to judge by the enthusiasm and sustained concentration of the class for nearly an hour, it was very successful) was dependent on two factors: a rich and challenging stimulus; and a highly skilled teacher, sensitive to the needs and abilities of all the pupils in the class.

References

Alexander, R. (2004). *Towards Dialogic Teaching: Rethinking Classroom Talk*. Cambridge: Dialogos

Sharwood Smith, J. E. (1977). *On Teaching Classics*. London: Routledge and Kegan Paul

7 Latin – the current situation

When we turn our attention to classics in secondary schools, we find that the position is almost exactly the opposite of that in primary schools. Whereas in the latter classics is part of the compulsory curriculum but taught almost entirely by non-specialists, in the former it has no place in the compulsory curriculum but – in schools where it is offered – is taught mostly by specialists. Even before the advent of the National Curriculum classical subjects in all types of secondary school were under considerable pressure because of a number of factors (two of which, lack of time and shortage of teachers, will be examined in detail in this chapter), but its introduction exacerbated an already difficult situation and left classics in maintained schools in a precarious position, with, at a conservative estimate, fewer than one in ten offering any classical subject to GCSE by 2003 (see pages 91–7).[1]

In 1996, when I was appointed Director of the Cambridge School Classics Project (CSCP), CSCP was faced with a dilemma: should its energies and efforts to promote Latin in schools be concentrated on continuing support for the relatively few schools still offering Latin or on the development of new ways to make Latin available in schools with no provision for the subject, i.e. the large majority of maintained schools? In the event, CSCP tried to do both. On the one hand, the revision of the Cambridge Latin Course (CLC), started in 1996 and completed in 2004, aimed to make the course more manageable for schools teaching Latin on ever-decreasing time allowances, primarily by shortening stories and reducing the vocabulary (Story 2003: 89). On the other hand, moves were made to widen access to Latin, building on the work already undertaken by Pat Story, the previous director, who had overseen the creation of independent learning manuals to

---

[1] On the positive side, Will Griffiths, the current Director of the Cambridge Schools Classics Project (CSCP), reports a growing number of maintained schools offering Latin as a taster at KS3, often as part of the school's gifted and talented programme, and we know that CLC Book 1 E-learning Resource has been bought by more than 170 schools with no classics teacher.

accompany the first two books of the CLC (Book I was published in 1992 and Book II in 1997) as a way of supporting pupils in schools with little or no access to a Latin teacher: in 1999 the decision was taken to run a pilot online Latin programme in two comprehensive schools (see chapter 9) and the following year the opportunity arose to develop a substantial bank of electronic resources for CLC Book I, which, it was hoped, would benefit learners whatever the classics provision in their school (see chapter 8). This chapter looks at the factors that led to the decision to develop online Latin courses.

The current state of Latin

How precarious is the position of Latin in secondary schools? When Martin Forrest discussed the state of classics in the wake of the introduction of the National Curriculum the only data available to him came from a survey undertaken by JACT in 1993 (in which the emphasis was on respondents' *perceptions* of the state of classics). The results showed that while 21 per cent of respondents expected an improvement over the next five years, 37.5 per cent believed that the situation would deteriorate (Forrest 1996: 144). The latter, sadly, proved correct on the evidence of examination entries in classical subjects at GCSE level. Entries in Latin have fallen significantly since the introduction of the National Curriculum, and, while overall entries for Greek[2] have remained fairly constant, closer examination reveals that entries from maintained schools have fallen even more sharply than equivalent entries for Latin.

Table 3   *Entries in GCSE Latin 1988 and 2005*

	Maintained comprehensive	Maintained grammar	Maintained secondary modern	Maintained post 16	Independent	Other	Total
1988	4,616	3,715	19	143	7,460	70	16,023
2005	1,707	1,586	0	95	6,340	15	9,743

Source: The Assessment and Qualifications Alliance (AQA) statistical division, Guildford, published by JACT

Table 4   *Entries in GCSE Greek 1988 and 2005*

	Maintained comprehensive	Maintained grammar	Maintained post 16	Independent	Other	Total
1988	112	334	27	821	26	1,320
2005	36	87	3	982	5	1,113

Source: AQA statistical division, Guildford, published by JACT

---

[2] Greek is used as a short-hand for classical Greek throughout this chapter.

Compared with the 1988 entry, the 2005 entry in GCSE Latin was down 63.0 per cent in comprehensive schools, 57.3 per cent in grammar schools and 15.0 per cent in independent schools (see table 3). For GCSE Greek, the figures are even more stark, with entries down by 67.8 per cent in comprehensive schools and 74.0 per cent in grammar schools, whereas in independent schools the entry was up by 19.6 per cent (see table 4).[3]

These changes have led to a significant shift in the balance of maintained/independent school entries at GCSE level. At the time when the GCSE was introduced, just over half of Latin entries (53 per cent) came from maintained schools and just under half (47 per cent) from independent schools, but by 2005 the maintained school share had dropped to just over a third (35 per cent) and the independent school share had risen to just under two thirds (65 per cent). The single most important factor behind this shift was the 1988 Education Reform Act, which introduced both local management of schools (which had financial implications for the resourcing of minority subjects) and the National Curriculum. The latter, in particular, had a significant impact on the provision of Latin: whereas independent schools were not required to adopt the National Curriculum, maintained schools had to remove, or reduce the time for, optional subjects, particularly at Key Stage 3, in order to ensure there was sufficient time to cover the compulsory curriculum as set out in the standing orders;[4] and the less time for teaching at Key Stage 3, the more difficult for teachers to persuade pupils to opt for a subject already perceived as being a difficult GCSE (see pages 97–8). In some schools Latin was retained by moving it off timetable, but this left the subject in direct competition with well-established extra-curricular options such as sport, music and drama, again making it difficult to recruit large numbers; and while this was an effective short-term expedient for keeping the subject alive, it left the subject more vulnerable to closure at short notice, for instance in the event of the classics teacher leaving.

Ofsted data on the 2003 GCSE entries, which gives information on 83 per cent of entries from maintained schools, provides a very detailed picture of the current state of classics. Of the approximately 3,000 maintained secondary schools in England,

---

[3] The Greek GCSE entry in 2005 was the highest for any year since the introduction of GCSEs in 1988. One contributory factor to the buoyant entries in Greek has been the publication of John Taylor's course (Taylor 2003), which is designed to enable schools to offer both classical languages to able linguists within the lesson allocation for Latin.

[4] When it was first introduced the National Curriculum comprised three core subjects (English, mathematics and science) and seven foundation subjects (art, geography, history, modern foreign languages, music, physical education and technology). Religious education was also compulsory. See Gay (2003) for further discussion of classics and the National Curriculum.

257 (86 grammar and 171 comprehensive) were listed as entering candidates in Latin, suggesting that fewer than one in ten maintained secondary schools offered Latin in 2003, compared with roughly one in four in 1988.[5] Worryingly for the longer-term viability of the subject, 11 per cent of the 257 schools entered a single candidate, 24 per cent fewer than five candidates, and 49 per cent fewer than ten candidates.

Another worrying aspect of the 2003 data is the uneven geographical spread of the schools offering Latin. There is a relatively high concentration of such schools in London and the South East, but there are very few in the North East, Yorkshire and Humber, South West and East Midlands, the figures for which emphasise the gravity of the situation. Of the 267 maintained secondary schools in the East Midlands – comprising Derbyshire, Leicestershire, Lincolnshire, Northamptonshire, Nottinghamshire and Rutland – only two comprehensives (out of 252), and seven grammar schools (out of fifteen) entered candidates for Latin; and eight of the nine schools were in one county, Lincolnshire, the only county in the East Midlands with grammar schools.

Table 5 *Maintained schools entering candidates for GCSEs in classical subjects in 2003, by region*

North East	10
North West	25
Yorkshire and the Humber	18
East Midlands	9
West Midlands	26
East of England	36
South East	73
South West	18
London	42
Total	257

Source: Ofsted

The uneven geographical spread of schools offering classics is also evident in the distribution of classics posts advertised in the *Times Educational Supplement*. For instance, in the academic year 2004/05, twenty-four maintained schools in England (0.8 per cent of maintained secondary schools) advertised full-time classics posts, of which fourteen were comprehensives and ten were grammar

[5] This figure is based on statistics given by Angela Rumbold in a statement to the House of Commons quoted by David Tristram (2003: 12).

schools; of these, thirteen were in the South East, only one in the West Country, and only four north of Birmingham.

The picture that emerges, then, is of a diminishing number of schools offering Latin, spread very unevenly across the English regions, with the subject, not surprisingly, much more likely to be available in regions that have retained a selective system. This decline in Latin provision since 1988 has been caused primarily by factors outside classicists' control, but there are steps which classicists themselves must take to enhance the chances of the subject's future survival in schools still offering Latin.

Latin on a shoe-string

A top priority for classicists should be the reform of the GCSE examination to ensure that it provides a realistic challenge for the average pupil in the average school,[6] given the time now available for the subject at Key Stages 3 and 4. This has been reduced to such an extent that many teachers can barely complete the examination syllabus by the end of Year 11, even when they take significant shortcuts. In the view of many teachers, the timetable allocation for Latin had already been pared back to the bare minimum long before the cuts triggered by the introduction of the National Curriculum. In fact, the inadequacy of the time allocated to Latin was one of the key issues that led to a review of the aims and syllabus of the O level Latin examination by the Classical Association in 1961:

> The Classical Association therefore decided to test the feelings of its members with a questionnaire. This was the underlying thought. Ever since Latin, instead of having the time-table as a royal residence, was obliged by reduced circumstances to move into one or two rooms, such curtailments of the Latin syllabus as there had been had all resolved themselves into progressive abbreviations of the original schedule. Had the time come to take stock of the entire situation and place accordingly? Was some qualitative change now called for in contrast with the inch-by-inch surrender that had resulted from past encroachments on the Latinist's time? It was clear that if some such change were desired the Examining Boards should be informed, so that the examination syllabuses could be attuned to the new pattern.
>
> (Melluish 1962: 42)

In the survey members were asked, inter alia, if a wider reading of considerable portions of authors was desirable and practicable.

---

[6] As is evident from the survey discussed on pages 94–5, this is an issue for many independent schools as well as the maintained sector.

Summing up responses to this question, Melluish reported that 'the contrast in this question between "desirable" and "practicable" was seized on almost everywhere. For so many teachers, teaching with one eye on the calendar and the other on the unfinished portion of the syllabus, the relentless tick of the clock haunts the lesson like the tap of the deathwatch beetle' (Melluish 1962: 44–5) and he concluded his report in his usual forthright way:

> You cannot teach Latin on a shoe-string. Too many schools in too many parts of the country are attempting to have Latin on the cheap, with an inadequate time-allowance. The Head who expects Latin to be taught in two double portions of two periods, because this squares up neatly with the alternative of Domestic Science or Woodwork, is a Head that wants seeing to.
>
> (Melluish 1962: 47)

In the same publication Charles Baty observed that Latin below the sixth form was 'one subject of many, very lucky if it gets five periods a week for five years' and argued that 'curtailment has often gone beyond the limit of safety' (Baty 1962: 12–13). A more detailed picture was given by Sydney Morris in *Viae Novae: New Techniques in Latin Teaching*:

> After their first two years of Latin, some 300 hours of classwork and homework, pupils are usually still working entirely on made-up Latin, have no, or little, grasp of subjunctive usages, are not, on the whole, able to translate out of, or into, Latin with any degree of accuracy. After four years of Latin, some 600 hours of work, translation into English is all too often halting, and translation from English into Latin inaccurate; either way it is all too frequently a jigsaw puzzle. The weaknesses of such generalisations about standards are notorious; but very many competent observers agree that there is little facility with the language on the part of the majority of the pupils, little confidence in their ability, scant feeling for what is right and wrong, little attack and less precision.
>
> (Morris 1966: 7–8)

One can only smile ruefully at such complaints about what seems now to be a remarkably generous time allocation compared with the situation today. A survey of twenty-five schools (five comprehensive, five grammar, fifteen independent) carried out in 2005 showed that the average length of Latin course from start to GCSE across all types of school was about 290 hours (excluding homework), and though this was a small and not altogether representative sample, one might conclude that, taking homework into account, the time allocation in

2005 was on average at least a third less than forty years earlier.[7] Among the survey schools the comprehensives and grammar schools had about 25 per cent less time than independent schools (245 hours as opposed to 325 hours), with significantly less time at Key Stage 3 but a comparable allocation at Key Stage 4. Most of the 11–18 independent schools in the survey (eleven out of thirteen) started Latin in Year 7, four of the five grammar schools started in Year 8 (the fifth school started in Year 7), and, of the five comprehensive schools, one started in Year 7, two in Year 8 and two in Year 9. The most generous time allowance was 390 hours (in a mixed independent school) and the least generous 210 hours (in a boys' grammar school).

No matter what the ability of the pupils or the size of the class, teaching Latin to GCSE in under 250 hours represents an unrealistic challenge, even with the reductions that have taken place in GCSE specifications since its introduction:

> [The time allocated to Latin in schools] has always varied, even between schools in the same sector, but over the last forty years it has shown some startling reductions ... In response to this situation GCSE boards have modified their syllabuses: the amount of required accidence, syntax and vocabulary has been reduced, as have the length of the prescribed texts and the number of cultural topics to be examined. Even so, teachers tend to omit the parts of the course that are designed to ease the transition to original Latin and struggle to initiate their students in literature that is linguistically and conceptually demanding. Nevertheless, they rightly argue that the reading of a selection of Catullus poems or part of a book of the *Aeneid* is a memorable experience and a fitting end to the course.
>
> (Story 2003: 90)

As Pat Story says, in spite of struggling to get pupils to a sufficiently high level of competence in the language to be able to read Latin literature in the original, classics teachers are strongly opposed to any changes in the GCSE that would involve the removal of the literature component. For many teachers, after all, that is the main justification for studying Latin, and was a major consideration in the overhaul of the O level syllabus in the wake of the Classical Association's review. Writing at that time, Dora Pym asserted that

a four-year course in the Main School, however it be examined,

---

[7] I carried out this survey as part of the consultation process for the QCA review of GCSE and A level criteria. Figures are only approximate as schools were asked to give hours per week but not asked how long their school year was. Figures given here are calculated on the basis of a thirty-five-week teaching year in maintained schools and a thirty-one-week teaching year in independent schools.

must be an end in itself, neither a foundation for something which will never be built nor an inferior version of specialist's Latin. Its aim and justification can only be an introduction to Latin literature; this experience must have quality and depth even if the amount of Latin read is not large.

(Pym 1962: 36)

However, this view was not shared by all classics teachers at the time. As Melluish pointed out,

set books have their supporters as well as their detractors, and it is difficult not to sympathize with the contentions of either side. Division largely runs between those who believe their first task to be that of teaching Latin as a language, and on the other hand those who feel that the learning of that language is not in itself justifiable unless it is employed in reading some small portion of the best Latin literature. The former point to the lavish expenditure of time in revising set books, and in some bad cases even learning translations off by heart; the latter refer to the evil of reading only 'snippets' of Latin, and point to the sense of solid achievement, often genuinely felt, by those who have really mastered some few hundred lines, say, of Virgil.

(Melluish 1962: 45)

Those who believed their first task was that of teaching Latin as a language may have lost the debate over the future shape of the O level, but might claim that their objections were largely justified, given the amount of time spent on set texts today and the methods used to teach and learn them.[8] The latter is a particular cause for concern: shortage of time means that most pupils do not acquire the linguistic competence or the experience of classical literature to cope with the demands of the GCSE without substantial spoon-feeding by the teacher; and the less time teachers have to cover the syllabus the more likely they are to resort to a dictated translation – and even a dictated commentary – in order to ensure that their pupils perform well in the examination; and both translation and commentary will be learnt by heart by conscientious pupils desperate to achieve an A grade. Without great skill on the part of the teacher, even the best passages from Virgil can feel like another 'chunk' to be swallowed whole rather than a piece of literature to be savoured and appreciated.

What should be done about it? In Melluish's words, is some qualitative change now called for in contrast with the inch-by-inch

---

[8] For a recent critique of set texts from a traditional standpoint see John Taylor (2005) who quotes a colleague's complaint that 'they spend so much time on set texts in the GCSE year that they forget all their Latin'.

surrender that has resulted from past encroachments on the Latinist's time (Melluish 1962: 42)? Do we need a major review of GCSE Latin? Pat Story wonders whether less able pupils on two- or three-year Latin courses would not be better served by 'an option in the GCSE examination ... which did not require the study of one or both set texts, but substituted an extra topic or literature in translation' (Story 2003: 91). With a review of the QCA criteria for GCSE subjects imminent and with only one examining board now offering Latin GCSE, at the time of writing there is a real opportunity to create a more realistic examination. But any radical changes such as introducing a literature topic in translation need the support from a wide range of teachers, and as yet attempts to trigger a national debate on the issue have met with only limited success (unlike the response to the Classical Association survey when 'well-attended meetings were held all over the country [and] numerous and lengthy postal replies were received' (Melluish 1962: 42–3)).

There is further evidence that action is needed urgently to make Latin GCSE more manageable. Research undertaken by Robert Coe at the Curriculum, Evaluation and Management Centre at the University of Durham examined the relative difficulty of thirty-four GCSE subjects based on the performance of 615,800 Year 11 pupils in summer 2004. The results showed that at grade C Latin was the most difficult of all thirty-four subjects, by some distance:

> At grade C ... Latin is about a grade harder than the next hardest subject, but even the next few subjects (statistics, chemistry, physics, Spanish) are about a grade harder than those at the other end of the scale (textiles, vocational science, vocational leisure and tourism, child development).
>
> (Coe 2006: 9)

As Coe is at pains to point out in his report, one needs to avoid a simplistic interpretation of the findings: subjects are ranked according to the difficulty of achieving the different grades, not according to the difficulty of the subject itself, and he suggests that there might be a number of reasons for one subject being ranked as more difficult than another:

> For example, if the only students who enter a particular subject are especially motivated in that subject, then the fact that they do well does not necessarily indicate that it was easier. This might be the case in Drama or vocational subjects, for example.
>
> At the other end of the scale, some subjects may often not be allocated the same timetable time as others, and hence students

may tend to do less well in these subjects than in their others. The GCSE examination itself may be no harder in that subject, but overall students tend to be less well prepared for it. Latin and statistics might be examples of such 'under-timetabled' subjects.

(Coe 2006: 11)

Whatever the reasons for Latin emerging as the most difficult subject, the findings reinforce a commonly held perception that Latin is a very difficult GCSE; and the fact that Latin may not be harder, merely 'under-timetabled', does not mean that steps should not be taken to make it more manageable. If we take no action, we will increase the chances of Latin disappearing from schools struggling each year to recruit a viable GCSE class.

Teaching posts and teacher supply

A further factor that threatens the survival of Latin in maintained schools and seriously limits the chances of any significant revival, is teacher supply. It is not that classics teachers are an ageing community, as was suggested by one student quoted by Judith Affleck (2003: 167):[9] in fact, since 1991 nearly 500 new, mostly young, teachers have entered the profession via the PGCE route alone. The main cause for concern is the shrinking number of suitably qualified applicants for classics posts. Evidence from two surveys of schools advertising classics posts, full-time and part-time, in the *Times Educational Supplement*, carried out in 1995 and 2002, shows a marked decline in appropriately qualified applicants and diminishing interest in posts in the maintained sector. Findings from the 2002 survey (based on returns from 115 out of 125 schools sent the survey) showed that only 20.9 per cent of posts, across all types of school, attracted a field of more than ten applicants, compared with 85.3 per cent in 1995 (when there were 75 returns from 89 schools); and only 31.3 per cent of headteachers in 2002 felt that the field of applicants was strong or very strong, compared with 66.8 per cent in 1995. Two comprehensives had no applicants, and only five maintained schools (out of 27) had more than five applicants. Although the headteacher of one comprehensive was sanguine about the position of classics ('classics has grown hugely at GCSE and AS/A2 in the last few years, esp. popular at GCSE for boys – great value added'), among the remainder the mood was pessimistic:

> We may not offer Latin in future if we remain unable to appoint a permanent replacement. We have asked our existing part-time

---

[9] The student was said to have commented that 'there are very, very few Latin teachers around, and those who are seem to be getting on a bit'!

teacher to cover the Latin timetable next year because of our failure to appoint a permanent replacement.

Since Sept. 4 part-timers have been and gone, unable to cope. Have now appointed 2 full-time teachers: one, qualified and experienced; the other, unqualified (except in Poland) and inexperienced.

3 enquiries, 1 applicant only. We are keen to maintain and enhance [classics], but the staffing situation at national level is very worrying.

The results of the 2002 survey suggest also that we are losing substantially more teachers from the profession than are entering it: of the 114 vacancies created in 2001–2, forty-six were created by teachers leaving classics teaching. In the same year thirty trainees successfully completed the PGCE, of whom twenty-eight went into teaching, leaving a net loss of eighteen classics teachers from the profession.[10] Yet the Training and Development Agency for Schools continues to cut PGCE places for classics. Since 1993, while there has been a steady increase in the number of posts advertised in the *Times Educational Supplement*, peaking with 151 posts in 2003, the

Table 6   *Ratio of PGCE graduates to advertised classics posts 1993–2006[a]*

Year	PGCE graduates	Classics posts	Jobs per graduate
1993	51	52	1.02
1994	47	69	1.47
1995	39	73	1.87
1996	40	61	1.56
1997	34	107	3.15
1998	33	102	3.09
1999	38	73	1.92
2000	21	111	5.29
2001	32	139	4.34
2002	30	141	4.70
2003	32	151	4.72
2004	34	150	4.41
2005	32	131	4.09
2006	28	145	5.18

[a] Only full-time posts of at least one year's duration are included.

[10] This does not take into account, of course, returners to teaching or people entering teaching without a qualification, although 80 per cent of successful applicants in 2002 had a classics PGCE.

number of teacher training places allocated to classics by the government has been steadily reduced, from more than fifty, spread across four training institutions,[11] in 1993 to only twenty-nine in 2006 (fifteen at Cambridge, fourteen at King's College London).

One reason for the large number of posts advertised in recent years has been the tendency of schools faced with a shortage of suitable candidates to make one-year appointments in the first instance (effectively a probationary year). This policy can lead to a very rapid turnover of staff: eleven maintained schools (five comprehensive and six grammar) have advertised at least four times in the last five years; and in the most extreme example a mixed grammar school ran eight advertisements in that period for classics posts, including three for head of department. Such unsettled staffing inevitably weakens the position of classics in the curriculum and makes it very difficult to engender the level of loyalty and commitment among pupils needed to create viable examination classes, the lack of which may have prevented some teachers from applying for the post in the first place.

There is now a serious danger of a downward spiral, with schools dropping Latin from the curriculum if they are unable to recruit classics staff, leading to fewer classicists from maintained schools on classical language courses at university, fewer therefore eligible for the PGCE and fewer newly qualified teachers likely to go into maintained schools. Although many PGCE trainees express a desire, when they embark on the course, to teach in the maintained sector, most end up working in the independent sector. There are a number of reasons for this. Firstly, many trainees are put off by the prospect of being the only full-time classicist in a school, as is often the case in the maintained sector, and starting their teaching career with sole responsibility for classics. Secondly, opportunities for career development within classics are very limited in maintained schools: classics is often subsumed within a larger faculty, either languages or humanities, and there may not even be a designated head of classics post. Thirdly, posts in the maintained sector are more likely to involve teaching a subject other than classics, sometimes for a significant proportion of the timetable. Fourthly, pay and conditions can be considerably more favourable in the independent than the maintained sector. Even when classicists do start their careers in the maintained sector, many move across to the independent sector within ten years. By way of illustration, of the 124 Cambridge trainees who entered the teaching profession

---

[11] The University of Nottingham closed its classics PGCE course in 1994, and St Mary's College, Twickenham, followed suit in 2002.

between 1992 and 2001, twenty-eight went into the maintained sector, of whom twelve are still teaching in the maintained sector, seven as heads of department; and of the ninety-six trainees who went into the independent sector only one subsequently moved to a maintained school.

So what is the long-term prognosis for classics in maintained secondary schools? Are there, as David Tristram says, 'some grounds for optimism' (Tristram 2003: 19) that Latin can be kept alive by the enthusiasm and dedication of classics teachers? If that is to be the case, classicists have to find ways of coping with the very limited time available to teach the subject to GCSE. As we shall see in the next chapter, a certain amount can be done to alleviate this problem through the use of information and communication technology (ICT) inside and outside the classroom. Nevertheless, without the creation of a GCSE examination that provides a more realistic challenge for pupils given the limited time available, there is a serious danger that many of the 49 per cent of the 257 maintained schools who ran GCSE Latin in 2003 with fewer than ten pupils may drop Latin from their GCSE options in the next five years (if they have not done so already); and we can expect searching questions from the enthusiastic and dedicated classics teachers in those schools about the appropriateness of the one remaining Latin GCSE. Even with the introduction of a new, more manageable GCSE, schools will not be able to offer Latin as an examination subject if they are unable to recruit, *and retain*, suitably qualified classics teachers. The question of teacher supply and retention is all the more worrying because now that there are no local authority advisers or HMIs with a dedicated classics brief, it is very hard to organise concerted action to address the issue at local, let alone national, level.

These issues highlight the importance of developing other ways, such as online courses, of providing access to Latin and to specialist support. Even if for most pupils an online course provides only a taster rather than a full GCSE course, it will still increase the chances of those pupils choosing to study Latin later. Recent government initiatives, such as Excellence in Cities, with its 'Gifted and Talented' strand, have created an environment in which schools have been willing to look again at subjects like Latin that offer something beyond the National Curriculum, and we know that there are many children and parents keen to see the subject being made available to them. CSCP has worked closely with the London borough of Barking and Dagenham to help introduce Latin into its eight secondary schools as part of its gifted and talented programme; and the most important factor in the success of the Latin clubs, according to a report by the local authority adviser responsible for the programme, was 'the enthusiasm of schools, headteachers, parents and pupils for the introduction of an initiative which would otherwise have been denied them' (Dyson 2003) – though the adviser might also have mentioned her own role in encouraging and supporting the schools and that of the LA in providing central funding for the initiative. Five years since the introduction of Latin, the Latin clubs are still run in Key Stage 3, and at Key Stage 4 Latin can be studied via video conference teaching by those wishing to take the subject to GCSE. Numbers are very small, but in a borough where there was no Latin whatsoever before 2001, this nevertheless represents a significant step forward. Meanwhile, another school, which began offering online Latin through CSCP in 1999, has recently created a part-time classics post to help establish classics more firmly in the curriculum, enabling it to offer Latin AS level for the first time, and already the possibility of starting Classical Civilisation has been discussed with the newly appointed teacher. Chapter 9 tracks the progress of the first online Latin cohort in this school from the first beginnings of the Cambridge Online Latin Project through to their GCSE examination. But first chapter 8 looks at the setting up of the Cambridge Online Latin Project and examines the use of ICT to enrich and enhance the teaching of the Cambridge Latin Course.

References

Affleck, J. (2003). 'Twilight classics', in Morwood, J. (ed.), *The Teaching of Classics*, pp. 159–69. Cambridge: Cambridge University Press

Baty, C. W. (1962). 'Classics in the schools', in *Re-appraisal: Some New Thoughts on the Teaching of Classics*, supplement to *Greece & Rome* IX(1), pp. 10–14. Oxford: Clarendon Press

Coe, R. (2006). 'Relative difficulties of examinations at GCSE: an application of the Rasch model'. Research paper, Curriculum, Evaluation and Management (CEM) Centre, University of Durham

Dyson, J. (2003). 'An evaluation of responses of gifted and talented students in a socially deprived urban area of London, United Kingdom, to involvement in the Cambridge Online Latin Project'. Paper given at the Annual Meeting of the American Educational Research Association for the Research into Giftedness and Talent, Chicago USA

Forrest, M. (1996). *Modernising the Classics: A Study in Curriculum Development*. Exeter: Exeter University Press

Gay, B. (2003). 'Classics teaching and the National Curriculum', in Morwood, J. (ed.), *The Teaching of Classics*, pp. 20–35. Cambridge: Cambridge University Press

Melluish, T. W. (1962). 'Latin enquiry', in *Re-appraisal: Some New Thoughts on the Teaching of Classics*, supplement to *Greece & Rome* IX(1), pp. 42–7. Oxford: Clarendon Press

Morris, S. (1966). *Viae Novae: New Techniques in Latin Teaching*. London: Hulton Educational Publications

Pym, D. (1962). 'The fig-tree', in *Re-appraisal: Some New Thoughts on the Teaching of Classics*, supplement to *Greece & Rome* IX(1), pp. 35–41. Oxford: Clarendon Press

Story, E. P. (2003). 'The development of the Cambridge Latin Course', in Morwood, J. (ed.), *The Teaching of Classics*, pp. 85–91. Cambridge: Cambridge University Press

Taylor, J. (2003). *Greek to GCSE, Part 1 and Part 2*. Bristol: Duckworth Classical Press

Taylor, J. (2005). 'The tyranny of set texts', *Journal of Classics Teaching* 3 (4), p. 11.

Tristram, D. (2003). 'Classics in the curriculum from the 1960s to the 1990s', in Morwood, J. (ed.), *The Teaching of Classics*, pp. 6–19. Cambridge: Cambridge University Press

8 | The Cambridge Latin Course in the digital age

Although the Cambridge School Classics Project (CSCP) began exploring possible uses of information and communication technology (ICT) in the teaching and learning of Latin in the late 1980s, it was only with the launch of the Cambridge Online Latin Project (COLP) that it began sustained ICT development, culminating in the creation of the Cambridge Latin Course (CLC) Book I E-learning Resource and the CSCP website and associated range of online services and support. COLP started out in 1999 as a very modest, low-budget project with the limited objective of exploring the feasibility of teaching Latin via the internet in two comprehensive schools in north Essex; but it quickly took on a life of its own when, in January 2000, a short article on the project was published on the front page of *The Times* newspaper. Under the heading 'Internet gives Latin lovers a new lease' it outlined the aims of COLP and gave the address of CSCP's website for people interested in finding out more. Within twenty-four hours more than 30,000 people had visited the website and within a month CSCP had received e-mails from more than a thousand would-be Latin scholars from all over the world (from Abu Dhabi to Thailand, from Albania to Zimbabwe) wanting to learn the language online. In most cases the correspondents already had experience of Latin. For some it was a chance to revive their knowledge:

> I am a Cambridge graduate (Egyptologist!), and with some time on my hands. I did Latin O level and also History with Foreign Texts double A level. This involved Latin classical and medieval texts. I have forgotten everything I ever knew but would like to revive some of that knowledge before I am too old.

For others it was a chance to make amends for past failures:

> At school (40 odd years ago) Latin was my best subject. I failed my O level twice. My Headmaster (who was also my Latin

master) was appalled. I now need to revitalise my interest in the Language.

In the short term they were to be disappointed[1] – COLP was set up initially with schools, not individuals, in mind – but the scale of the response highlighted the extent of interest in Latin and the potential of modern technology to reach out to a global market.[2] In the same edition of *The Times*, a leading article, 'Latin online – welcome back Mr Chips', enthusiastically trumpeted the benefits of the digital age for classics:

> Silicon is the latest style in school. Binary codes have ousted the abacus. Hard drives are performing the pedagogue's task. Who wants a blackboard when they can plug in a notebook? Who needs a blackboard where there is a databank instead? The Internet can serve as a textbook. Lessons can be conducted on-line. Homework can be modemed, excuses can be e-mailed, corrections can easily be electronically filed. No wonder that the modern Mr Chips is taking advantage of technology, or that classrooms are expanding into cyberspace – and, what is more, time-travelling back to Virgil and the Trojan War.
>
> ... Not every school is fortunate enough to have inspiring or experienced teachers – especially in the more specialist subjects. But now every pupil could have at their fingertips their own pedagogue-on-disk, delivering lessons in byte-sized chunks to be digested and assimilated at the rate best suited to the individual. Of course DOS will never weed out the dossers. The lazy can give themselves an exeat at the touch of an exit button, type out their detention lines at a flick of the copy-and-paste keys. But for the enthusiast technology will surely work to translate the teaching of this 'dead' language into a relevant modern realm. All they will need to do if they want to learn Latin is bring in an Apple for Mr Chips.
>
> (*The Times*, 31 January 2000)

This high-profile publicity coincided with an announcement by Michael Wills, the Minister of State for ICT in Schools, of a £5 million Key Stage 3 Educational Service Pilot (hereafter referred to as the DfEE KS3 pilot) to develop ICT-based courses in mathematics, Latin and Japanese. The aims of the pilot were threefold: to raise standards; to widen access to subjects; and to address teacher shortages. With

---

[1] But some later joined a pilot course for independent learners, including the Cambridge Egyptologist who, by the time she completed her online studies four years later, had read most of Tacitus *Annals* IV with an e-tutor.

[2] The first group of online independent learners I taught comprised a retired doctor from Australia, a lawyer from the Virgin Islands and a general practitioner from Weston-super-Mare.

specific reference to classics the hope was expressed in the prospectus issued by the Department for Education and Employment (DfEE) that the projects would expand opportunities for Key Stage 3 pupils in a number of ways including 'reviving interest in the classics by providing challenging, stimulating teaching in a way that will appeal to a new generation' (DfEE 2000: 3).

Five months later the Cambridge School Classics Project was part of the consortium (with Granada Media[3] and Cambridge University Press) that was awarded the contract for Latin. The brief was to create and pilot a one-year KS3 Latin course for pupils in schools (with or without a Latin specialist teacher) and for independent learners, the work to be completed within the academic year 2000/01. CSCP was responsible for designing the three separate courses for the different types of learner and for advising on the content of the electronic resources; Granada Media, the lead partner in the consortium, oversaw the creation of these resources and all other technical aspects of the pilot; and Cambridge University Press designed and produced all print materials. By October 2000 twelve e-tutors were working for COLP, teaching 335 pupils in sixteen schools with no Latin teacher, in locations as far apart as Tyneside and Hampshire, Shropshire and Kent. At the same time a team of subject specialists started work on the development and creation of more than a thousand electronic items for CLC Book I, which were then distributed on CD to pilot schools between January and June 2001, at the rate of one Stage (i.e. chapter) every two weeks.[4]

Laying the foundations

CSCP's first electronic resources for the CLC, a disk of exercises and games to accompany Unit I[5] released in 1991, had been only moderately successful: although pupils enjoyed such activities as discovering their own fate (in Latin) in the eruption of Vesuvius '[the disk's] use was never widespread because of technical problems with computers or simply the difficulty of getting access to a computer room at the right time' (Story 2003: 88) – two issues still preventing effective use of ICT resources ten years later. A series of major publishing commitments precluded the possibility of any further software development for the remainder of the 1990s but by 1999, with the revision of the CLC well under way, and COLP about to begin, it

---

[3] Technically the contract was awarded to Granada Result, an off-shoot of Granada Media created specifically to carry out the work on the DfEE pilot.
[4] These pilot materials were then brought together on a single DVD, the CLC Book I E-Learning Resource. For a detailed description of the E-Learning Resource see Griffiths 2005.
[5] Before the publication of the fourth edition, the CLC textbooks were called Units rather than Books.

was an opportune time to start serious development of ICT resources. The DfEE pilot could not have come at a more opportune moment and marked a logical step forward in the continuing evolution of the CLC.[6]

In the first half of the 1990s Pat Story, the Director of CSCP at the time, was responsible for developing, and was joint author of, two new publications which laid the foundations for much of the work undertaken ten years later on the DfEE pilot. Firstly, she was co-author, with Jean Hubbard, of the CLC Units I and II Independent Learning Manuals in response to what she described as 'the urgent need to evolve methods and produce materials which would enable students to work independently with only occasional help from the teacher' (Story 2003: 88). Although these manuals were published in book format, from the start the authors were aware of possible advantages of a digital version, particularly in terms of flexibility. The need for flexibility had been apparent when working on the answer books to accompany the independent learning manuals:

> Where understanding of stories is tested by comprehension questions, the Answer Book contains the answers to the questions only and not a translation of the story as well. To give a translation would seem to invalidate the comprehension exercises, but not to do so may cause problems to students who will want to know why their answer to a particular comprehension is wrong.

> Such problems could be alleviated if some or all of the Manual were put on computer. Students (or their teachers) could control the amount of help they were given by accessing only the information they wanted at any one time. The whole Course could in fact be treated more flexibly if it were computerised and it may be the next step to take.

> (Story 1993: 8)

Secondly, she worked with a team of three experienced teachers to produce Worksheet Masters, folders of photocopiable A4 worksheets for CLC Units I and II. These resource banks brought together a range of language consolidation, language awareness and aural comprehension exercises along with the exercises to extend and test knowledge of the cultural background. The materials, the majority of which were based on ideas contributed by practising teachers and had already been tried and tested in the classroom, were imaginative, highly visual and very well suited for adapting to electronic format.

---

[6] For a full account of the first twenty-five years of the CLC see Forrest 1996, chapters 5 and 9. For more recent developments see Story 2003.

In the second half of the 1990s much of CSCP's time was taken up by a full revision of the CLC, again under Pat Story's editorial control. This was a major undertaking, involving six separate publications for each of the first two books of the course alone.[7] The shift to a colour edition led to the integration of photographs that had previously been available only as slides in the main body of the textbook and also to the use of a large number of new photographs to enhance the revised cultural background sections. But from the point of view of the DfEE pilot, the most important aspect of the CLC revision lay not so much in the changes made to the content and appearance of the course as in the revision process itself, which involved the digitisation of all content, text and graphics, and the use of a morphological analyser to help with the editing of the text: this prosaically named software program was to play a key role in the subsequent development of electronic resources. This was not, in fact, the first time that CSCP used this sort of software. In the early 1980s the Linguistic and Literary Computer Centre in Cambridge created a language analyser specifically to help with the editing of the second edition of the CLC. This provided an alphabetical listing of all words in each Unit, giving each occurrence together with the context in which it occurred.

The new morphological analyser had its origins in a small-scale project, set up in 1992 with funding from the University of Cambridge Faculty of Classics, to explore the use of electronic texts to support undergraduates' independent study of prescribed texts. The aim of the project was to develop an electronic version of the longest and in many ways most challenging first-year text, Tacitus *Annals* IV, to speed up the translation process for students who, according to figures collected in a small-scale survey, spent approximately 70 per cent of their time when working on texts looking up words in the dictionary or grammar book and only 30 per cent reading the Latin. Work in this field was already ongoing in America both in California, at the Packard Humanities Institute, and in Boston, where the Perseus Project had developed a morphological analyser. A project in the Department of Classics in Manchester, Project Construe, had also been set up in the late 1980s with funding from the Computers in Teaching Initiative to conduct research into computer-based techniques for studying and teaching ancient Greek. A major component of this project was the development of an interactive morphological analyser for classical and New

---

[7] For each Book there is the main textbook, a *Teacher's Guide*, an *Independent Learning Manual* (now called the *Student Study Book*), an *Independent Learning Manual Answer Book*, a folder of Worksheet Masters and a Graded Test booklet.

Testament Greek. This was created by Tony Smith, a classics teacher turned computer programmer, who explained what the analyser did in the following terms:

> It uses tables of stems and endings (and a number of exceptions that cannot be treated easily by rule): particular sets of endings are only acceptable with particular types of stem. A word for analysis is examined from both ends to see what possible combinations of stems and endings can be found. The program then produces the list of possible analyses it has discovered. If there are accents indicated in the word they are used to decide the likelihood of a given analysis, but an incorrect or missing accent does not prevent an analysis being made. Breathings and iota subscripts are assumed to be correct.
>
> (Tony Smith, private correspondence with the author)

Even though Latin provides fewer challenges than Greek, it took four years of adjustment and refinement to make the tables needed for the analyser ready for use not merely with Tacitus *Annals* IV but with the full range of authors from the classical period. Once work began on the fourth edition of the CLC in 1996, it quickly became apparent that this analyser, which had been developed as a learning tool for undergraduates, could also be a very powerful, time-saving tool for the CLC revision team. Since a main aim of the revision was to shorten the stories to enable pupils to work through the course more quickly, it was essential to be able to track the 'history' of every word removed during the revision, since the removal of a sentence, a phrase or even a single word, could have a knock-on effect for the glossing of words in stories and the compiling of the full vocabulary at the back of each book. With the aid of the analyser it was possible to generate automatically the history of every headword in any given story across the whole of the CLC, showing when a word occurred for the first time, how many times it occurred, and in what forms.[8] As well as being used for this behind-the-scenes revision task, in time the morphological analyser became the engine for a range of electronic resources, including vocabulary testers, the electronic version of the *Pocket Oxford Latin Dictionary*, electronic editions of texts from Cambridge University Press's Greek and Latin Classics series,[9] and the story exploring tool for CLC Book I, which we will consider in close detail later.

---

[8] A headword is the word under which a set of related dictionary definitions are listed; for example, *fero* is the headword for *ferebant*, *tulisse*, etc.

[9] The Cambridge Greek and Latin Classics, known popularly as the Green and Yellow series, is a selection of classical texts, Latin and Greek, with commentaries designed for the undergraduate market.

Enhancing the history and culture

Given the issues facing Latin identified in the previous chapter CSCP had clear priorities for the development of electronic resources for the DfEE KS3 pilot: with a view to stimulating recruitment, the new materials needed to be appealing and engaging, allowing flexible access (for use in schools with or without a classics specialist) and providing time-saving pathways through the course. These priorities overlapped in many ways with those of the DfEE as outlined in their prospectus for the KS3 pilot. Their requirements for the pilot service (i.e. the electronic courses and associated resources) in each subject were that it should, inter alia,

> be exciting and fun to use without losing sight of educational focus;

> be innovative, utilising the full range of interactive technologies available in the classroom and the home;

> be suitable for use in both school and home environments, with or without teacher mediation.

(DfEE 2000: 3)

A starting point for discussion at initial planning meetings for the DfEE KS3 pilot was the relationship between the existing print materials and the proposed electronic resources, and from an early stage the view that the latter might entirely replace the former[10] was rejected for a number of reasons: in particular, the textbook did not require a power source (let alone a computer or an internet connection); was reassuringly familiar in design and layout; and contained, in a manageable and tangible form, the whole year's course.

Nevertheless, electronic resources could clearly bring significant enhancements to CLC Book I, particularly with respect to audio-visual materials. Teachers of the CLC had always been encouraged to employ a wide range of media in the classroom, and from the early 1970s audio-tapes (initially reel-to-reel and then cassettes) and slide sets (and later film-strips) had been an integral element of the CLC's support materials. But by the late 1990s the original slide sets were no longer available and demand for the film-strips had begun to fall away. Anecdotal evidence suggested that even where classics departments had the slides or film-strips they were rarely used by teachers, partly because of problems with access to and setting up of equipment; partly because of shortage of time; and partly because the fourth edition of the CLC, with its wealth of colour illustrations, in many ways had rendered the slides and film-strips redundant. As

---

[10] A view expressed in the leader in *The Times*, 31 January 2000, 'The Internet can serve as a textbook'.

far as audio-tapes were concerned, although teachers acknowledged the value of pupils hearing the Latin stories read aloud, they were increasingly reluctant to set aside their limited teaching time for listening activities. Granada Media was happy to devote a significant proportion of the budget to the creation of audio-visual materials as it played to their strengths – and they liked the idea of giving Caecilius and family the Coronation Street treatment.

As a result a wide and comprehensive range of audio-visual materials was developed for the DfEE KS3 pilot, including audio versions of every story in CLC Book I, as well as more than five hours of video footage, ranging from dramatisations of stories and 'talking head' explanations of points of grammar to a range of short videos on the history, culture and archaeology of Pompeii and Herculaneum and historical re-enactments. With all the audio-visual resources specially commissioned for the pilot, the cultural materials could be tailored to meet narrowly defined learning objectives specific to the context of CLC Book I and packaged as mini-documentaries, mostly less than five minutes long. Apart from other considerations it was hoped that presenting information in this way would save a great deal of time for teachers used to trawling commercially available resources to locate the three-minute section most relevant to their lesson on, say, the baths or gladiatorial shows.

The audio-visual resources proved a great success with pupils in the pilot schools with no Latin teacher. In their feedback they provided a salutary reminder of the value and importance of the spoken word in the Latin classroom, commenting very favourably on the way the audio materials added to their feel for Latin as a living language:

> Hearing is important; it helps with pronunciation. You get a feel for the language.

> It is more fun now. Before I thought of Latin as a church language and now it is more like a real language. People did actually speak fluently in Latin.

But it was the video clips that pupils enjoyed most. They liked both the factual documentaries (twelve months after the release of the film *Gladiator*, the clips about gladiators and gladiatorial shows were still particularly popular) and the dramatisations of the stories, which they felt enhanced their understanding of the main characters from Book I (one pupil said that she had found the dramatisations helpful because 'you can tell a lot about the characters judging from their facial expressions. Metella, for instance, seems to be a bit snobbish'). There was less agreement, on the other hand, about the instructional clips of a teacher talking through new points of grammar: while some pupils found the video explanations helpful, others found them confusing. But the audio-visual resources generally engaged and motivated pupils; and with the materials available on the school network and on CD, pupils who missed Latin club could still listen to the story or watch the video they missed before the next session. In short, the pupils' learning experience was significantly enriched.

Speeding up the reading process

Having looked at one of the more obviously motivational elements of the CLC electronic resources, we now turn to an electronic resource designed to help pupils' language acquisition and speed up their reading and translation of the stories, which form such a central part of the CLC. In addition to interactive activities, such as sorting and gap-filling exercises and vocabulary testing, the DfEE KS3 pilot materials included an electronic version of every story in CLC Book I, with each word in the story linked through to its dictionary definition as given at the back of the textbook (the morphological analyser at work again). In the example shown in figure 4, clicking on *tacuērunt* has brought up '**tacet** is silent, is quiet', and has also given the perfect of the verb, again as listed in the back of the textbook. But what might have taken the learner 15–20 seconds to find in the textbook appears instantly on the computer screen. The aim of this 'quick-click' look-up facility was to improve the acquisition and consolidation of vocabulary by increasing the frequency with which pupils encountered any given word in context (Griffiths 2005: 11); to enhance pupils' understanding and enjoyment of the story by engagement with the text at phrase and sentence, as well as at word, level; and thereby help sustain motivation.

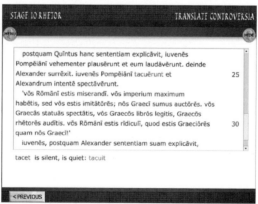

Figure 4 *Screen dump from the electronic resource for CLC Book I; reproduced with permission of the Cambridge School Classics Project*

The quick-click look-up tool has proved very popular. Since the stories have been made available with this facility on the CSCP website, they have regularly been amongst the most commonly used resources, along with vocabulary testers: in the week after half term in June 2006 quick-click look-up stories were visited 9,310 times (and the vocabulary testers 9,397 times), out of a total of 58,401 visits to the site as a whole during that week.

An investigation into pupils' use of and attitude towards the quick-click look-up facility was carried out by Tenley Laserson in 2005 as part of a wider examination of pupils' use of CSCP's website resources in three schools with no Latin teacher. When pupils were asked in an attitudinal questionnaire how helpful they found the quick-click look-up, their responses were as follows:

Never used it	1
Not helpful	2
Fairly helpful	3
Helpful	8
Very helpful	33

And when they were asked to say whether they preferred using the textbook or electronic resources when translating, their responses revealed that

> a clear majority of students not only prefer to use electronic resources when they translate (67 per cent), but in so doing, they believe that they translate faster (68 per cent), more accurately (62 per cent), with a better understanding of the plot (61 per cent) and Latin grammar (65 per cent).
>
> (Laserson 2005: 44)[11]

But in spite of having a clear preference for using the electronic resources rather than the textbook when translating stories, and in spite of believing that using the electronic resources improved the accuracy of their translation and understanding of plot and grammar, many pupils were uneasy about using the electronic resources rather than using the textbook, even though they were aware that the quick-click look-up and the dictionary at the back of the textbook provided exactly the same information. While they appreciated the extent to which the quick-click look-up removed the drudgery, the fact that it did so made them feel that when they were

---

[11] Of course these results show only pupils' *perceptions* of the value of quick-click look-up; and while they were in a position to judge the speed at which they translated the stories, only a Latin teacher would be able to assess the accuracy of their translation, or their understanding of plot and grammar.

using it they were not doing 'real' work:

> You just click the button and it will give you the answer so you're not really translating yourself.

> It's an arduous process and we could do it in a minute on the computer. But I actually think you learn better if you do it from the book.

> You use more of your mind when you translate from the book. The CSCP website is too easy.

> I think [the textbook] is better for learning because on the computer you click on the words and it tells you, but in the textbook you work it out.

Laserson cites other research into pupils' perspectives on the contribution of ICT to learning which found similar concerns among pupils about technology providing shortcuts:

> We were struck that, whilst pupils acknowledged ways in which technology could facilitate production of their work – effecting tasks and enabling refinements, they rarely perceived these as directly benefiting learning: 'it doesn't help you learn'. They expressed similar reservations about using technology, where they saw it providing a fast track that by-passed opportunities for mental processing and challenge (e.g. in Maths).
> (Deaney, Ruthven and Hennessy 2003: 162; cited in Laserson 2005: 61)

Pupils taking part in Laserson's research clearly had misgivings about the quality of their learning when using electronic aids, and when asked what they thought about having an entirely computer-based course they showed 'a staunch and rather traditional attachment to the book' (Laserson 2005: 54). As one pupil put it, 'if you didn't have the book, it wouldn't be Latin'; and another perceptively commented that 'You have to really keep the books otherwise people would lose interest. If you don't have, like, structure ... I mean, like, on computers you can really go into anything you want, but if you have a structure, people learn better.' In addition to the structure provided by the textbook, Laserson suggests that pupils appreciate its physical permanence, as opposed to the ephemeral nature of computer materials, and 'its portability, the ability to refer back to it at any time (in class, outside class, at home) and anywhere (bedroom, kitchen, school hallway). In addition, its linear structure makes it both easy to use and provides reliability and consistency (e.g. charts will always be at the back, new words are always at the end of a stage)' (Laserson 2005: 64).

Summing up the tension between pupils' preference for using the electronic resources and their reservations about their value as a learning tool, Laserson argues that

> data from both the questionnaire and semi-structured interviews suggest that students possess a model for language acquisition in which the process of acquiring information is as critical as the information itself. According to students, the process of 'real' learning demands time and labour – looking words up at the back of the textbook, writing out translations and memorising vocabulary.
>
> (Laserson 2005: 61)

The fact that pupils question the extent to which they are learning when they use the quick-click look-up does not mean that the tool is not useful, but it suggests that they need to be made aware of the potential value of the tool. They must learn to be discriminating in their use of it; and in fact feedback from students showed that 'while they may over-use this facility at first, as they progress through the course they use it more selectively' (Griffiths 2005: 11). One boy on the DfEE KS3 pilot said that he was not tempted to click on every word and in fact liked to challenge himself to check only one word per paragraph. This is the exception rather than the rule, however, and for most pupils, who find translating stories a slow process ('translations take forever', one pupil complained wearily), even with the electronic resources to help them, the quick-click look-up remains much used – and rightly so when pupils are reading a story for general sense and to find out more about the characters rather than as a thinly veiled grammar exercise. The CLC does include a great deal of reading material and pupils, particularly those learning Latin online, may spend much time preparing word-by-word translations of stories: whereas pupils with a Latin teacher will be exposed to a range of different approaches to stories designed to engage and motivate them, pupils learning Latin with an e-tutor are likely to have a relatively narrow choice of activities when working on stories, with translation very commonly set as a task, not least because it is, in practical terms, one of the easiest ways for the e-tutor to check that pupils have actually read the stories.

Laserson's research provides a useful reminder of the limitations as well as the benefits of ICT in language learning. It also highlights the need for explicit discussion with pupils about the role and value of ICT in supporting their learning so that they can become mature, sophisticated users of ICT. This is already a requirement of standing orders for ICT at Key Stage 4, in which it is stated that pupils should be taught 'to be discriminating in their use of information sources and ICT tools' and to 'evaluate the effectiveness of their own and others' uses of information sources and ICT tools, using the results to improve the quality of their work and to inform future judgements' (DfEE/QCA 1999: 22). In the same way that pupils need to learn to be discriminating users of the internet, able to make sound critical judgements about the status and reliability of information on the web, so they need to be taught to be responsible users of electronic tools such as the quick-click look-up and to make informed decisions about which tools are appropriate for different tasks. Also the notion that 'real' learning cannot take place without hard graft needs to be challenged, particularly when it comes to vocabulary acquisition. It is not the amount of effort pupils put into locating a word that determines whether they will remember it: it is partly the thought they put into working out from the context what it might mean *before* they look it up, and partly the strategies they employ for moving it into their long-term memory *after* they have found out what the word means (for instance, making links with words they already know).

ICT and whole-class teaching

Thus far I have considered ways in which electronic resources can support pupils learning Latin with an e-tutor when working individually at a computer. Although the DfEE KS3 pilot was concerned primarily with this type of pupil, five schools where Latin was taught by a specialist teacher within the KS3 curriculum[12] also took part in the pilot and provided evidence of the way electronic resources could contribute to whole-class teaching.[13] With their experience of teaching Latin both with and without electronic resources, the specialist teachers' comments were most useful in identifying the potential benefits and drawbacks of ICT resources in the Latin classroom.

For the five specialist teachers involvement in the DfEE KS3 pilot provided an opportunity to use ICT equipment which was not, at the time, commonly available in schools: they were each given a laptop with the pilot software pre-loaded and also a data projector if the school did not already have one.[14] The simple and obvious move of

---

[12] In one school Latin was offered off-timetable by a specialist teacher as an enrichment activity.
[13] Because of technical problems the specialist teacher in one school was unable to use the electronic resources regularly enough to complete the research questionnaires, so the findings discussed here are based on evidence from only four teachers.
[14] In 2000 data projectors were only just becoming sufficiently cheap, powerful and reliable for general classroom use. The alternative technology, at the start of the DfEE KS3 pilot, was interactive television, which was being promoted at the time as the most effective medium for using ICT in whole-class teaching and for accessing the internet in the home; but the technology soon proved unreliable and impractical with large classes.

providing the teachers with their own equipment transformed their approach to ICT: they no longer had to take classes to the computer suite but could use the ICT resources in their own classroom – and this immediately increased the amount that they used the resources; and they had much greater opportunity to familiarise themselves with the software and to explore the electronic resources on the laptops at home, and this in turn meant that they were more confident about using the resources in the classroom. It also led to a more positive attitude to ICT generally, as was evident from their responses to a questionnaire at the end of the DfEE KS3 pilot. Asked to what extent using the electronic resources had led to an improvement in their own ICT competence, the teachers said:[15]

> To a large extent. I'm sure that my confidence will increase when ... I use the resources next year.

> I have learnt an enormous amount about installation problems and how to resolve them! This has also been a good introduction to using a data projector – I didn't know what they were before!

> [my competence has] improved drastically this year and I am much more confident about using ICT in the classroom.

> <u>Lots</u> – I'm really excited about using it more, and seeing the improvement in pupils' motivation has made me realise how useful it will be. (teacher's emphasis)

For all of them, with the survival of Latin so dependent on successful recruitment of Year 9 pupils onto the GCSE course, the impact of ICT on pupil motivation was critical. When asked the extent to which the use of the electronic resources had affected pupils' motivation, the teachers answered in very positive terms, and were particularly pleased with the impact of the materials on lower achievers and potentially disaffected pupils:

> Hugely – they are all still really keen even though most won't be doing Latin to GCSE.

> [The materials have provided] success for weaker students on some exercises where they work through on their own, picking out examples – they are not shown up publicly if they get it wrong, and can get it right in private.

> The naughtier and less able students have responded well to them.

---

[15] All comments from specialist teachers cited on pages 117–19 are taken from a questionnaire conducted at the end of the DfEE pilot, July 2001.

Very motivating, especially for those who managed to use the CD Roms at home. They are keen enough to continue attending at 8.00 in the morning and at lunchtime ... In the case of one boy of lowish ability, his performance in other subjects has rocketed in the SATs and in Modern Languages. He has been a very interested and diligent student of Latin and I'm sure the systematic and motivating materials have boosted his confidence and overall level of achievement.

Increased motivation came not only from the rich and varied resources themselves (once again the video clips were particularly popular) but also from the opportunities the resources provided for class discussion. One teacher felt that the video clips made pupils more inquisitive and triggered 'more pertinent and more probing questions'; another that 'while watching video clips individuals have shone with their intelligent questions. They have become more confident in taking risks with their knowledge and learning.'

In all the schools the teacher had to set up and put away the computer equipment each lesson. Although this was time-consuming and meant the loss of five minutes at the beginning and end of each lesson, the teachers felt that the potential benefits of the electronic resources made it worthwhile. The data projector provided a central focus for the whole class in the same way as an overhead projector, but with the added benefit that it also fulfilled the functions of a slide projector and tape player, enabling the teacher to make full use of the computer's multimedia capabilities and extend the range of activities and approaches they could employ in lessons. The central focus was valued most by teachers when they were working with the class on Latin stories. With the text on screen, and quick-click look-up available, it was much easier to sustain the interest of lower achievers and less well motivated pupils, and at the same time it helped improve their understanding of the Latin: one teacher noted that the pupils had developed 'a more deductive way of understanding the grammar using stories on the screen, picking out details with the cursor, spotting forms and working out functions'. But, as with *War with Troy* (see pages 45–8), it was through *hearing* the stories that pupils gained most, partly because the regular use of audio material encouraged a less text-based approach to classroom teaching generally:

> The students have learnt to listen to Latin carefully because of the extensive use of audio on the course. They have also developed a desire to read Latin themselves and use their knowledge of the language more confidently.

Certainly they are less reliant on their written responses and are becoming more confident orally to explore [the stories] with each other. Therefore their learning strategies are more independent and co-operative.

All four teachers identified ways in which using the electronic resources had led to increased collaboration among pupils. In one school this had been most evident when the pupils worked in the computer suite and those who were more ICT literate (not necessarily the best Latin students) could act as expert helpers; in another school, a teacher noted that 'because of increased motivation classes have gelled well together [and there have been] lots of whole-class discussions to which all can contribute'. The wide range of electronic resources gave apparently weaker pupils more opportunity to demonstrate what they could do rather than what they could *not* do: this in turn gave them greater confidence to engage in class discussion. There was less consensus among the teachers, however, about other ways in which regular use of ICT had changed the classroom dynamics and helped pupils become more independent learners. Although one teacher indicated that her pupils had begun to take more responsibility for their learning, coming up with their own suggestions about what activities they would like to do (for instance, they suggested that they should 'learn and act out a play using the video conference facility, and make a copy on their own disc [and make] a database of vocab'), generally the teachers found that pupils still turned to them for help and guidance. Interestingly, when asked to what extent the use of the electronic resources had led to a change in their role in the classroom, from 'sage on the stage' to 'guide on the side', there was no clear agreement among the teachers:

> I am certainly no longer the source of all knowledge – the laptop has taken that role! Students did use me as a guide when they needed assistance. I would 'prompt' from the sidelines.

> Bizarrely, more sage on the stage but again next year would envisage guide.

> It is interesting that in lessons when we don't use the resources, I revert to sage on the stage! In Lab lessons in particular I am definitely a facilitator and guide.

> I'm not sure it has! The students are aware that the computer has a lot of the answers, but still turn to me for advice and assistance. The students feel they can advise me on anything to do with the computers without being cheeky!

Overall, the evidence from the admittedly small group of Latin teachers involved with the DfEE KS3 pilot was that the electronic resources brought considerable enhancements to whole-class teaching without in any way threatening to make teachers redundant, a concern expressed by many teachers alarmed by the more ambitious claims of the ICT lobby.

At the time of writing, five years on from the DfEE KS3 pilot, the electronic materials are available as the CLC Book I E-Learning Resource, on a single DVD instead of the twelve separate CDs on which they were originally issued (mirroring the development of the original Unit I print materials from twelve self-contained pamphlets and accompanying language information booklet into a single volume). Much of the value of the DVD lies in the exploitation of the computer's potential as a multimedia 'console', which provides a blend of audio-visual as well as textual resources, making it easier for teachers to cater for a wide range of learning styles in the Latin classroom and thereby open up the subject to pupils beyond a narrow band of very able linguists. In terms of the DfEE's original aims for the pilot the resources have undoubtedly encouraged 'challenging, stimulating teaching in a way that [appeals] to a new generation' and have had a significant impact on the engagement and motivation of pupils, particularly lower achievers. But in terms of addressing the shortage of time for teaching Latin, it is not clear whether the materials make it easier for pupils to cover the course more quickly: with so many materials available, it could actually take longer to cover Book I with the DVD than with the textbook alone. On the other hand, because many of the text-based resources are also available on the CSCP website, it is now more realistic to set pupils work to do at home that they could have tackled previously only in lesson time.

As for the claim in *The Times* that 'the Internet can serve as a textbook', the evidence of the DfEE KS3 pilot, and Tenley Laserson's research, suggests otherwise. When pupils were asked at the end of the DfEE KS3 pilot whether they agreed or not with the statement, 'I find that I learn better from a printed textbook than using the electronic resources', while 59 per cent disagreed and 11 percent expressed no preference, 29 per cent agreed. Electronic resources significantly enhance the textbook, but many pupils still attach great value to traditional resources, and effective learning (and teaching) is likely to draw on a blend of both traditional and new media to cater for the wide range of needs and interests to be found in most classrooms.

References

Deaney, R., Ruthven, K. and Hennessy, S. (2003). 'Pupil perspectives on the contribution of information and communication technology to teaching and learning in the secondary school', *Research Papers in Education* 18(2), pp. 141–65

DfEE (2000). *The Key Stage 3 Educational Service Pilot: Prospectus.* London: DfEE

DfEE/QCA (1999). *The National Curriculum for England: Information and Communication Technology.* London: DfEE/QCA

Forrest, M. (1996). *Modernising the Classics: A Study in Curriculum Development.* Exeter: Exeter University Press

Griffiths, W. (2005). 'Increasing access to Latin'. Paper given at international meeting of Latin teachers, Cambridge UK, July 2005. Available as download from www.cambridge.org/latinconference05; last accessed 2 December 2006

Laserson, T. (2005). 'To what extent can electronic resources enhance the study of Latin?'. MPhil thesis, University of Cambridge Faculty of Education

Story, E. P. (1993). 'Independent learning and the Cambridge Latin Course', *JACT Review* 2(14), pp. 7–8

Story, E. P. (2003). 'The development of the Cambridge Latin Course', in Morwood, J. (ed.), *The Teaching of Classics*, pp. 85–91. Cambridge: Cambridge University Press

9 | Latin in the virtual classroom

As was noted at the beginning of chapter 8 a key aim of the DfEE KS3 pilot was to investigate the contribution to learning that ICT-delivered courses could make in subject areas where there were teacher shortages (DfEE 2000: 2).[1] This was an issue of particular interest to the Cambridge School Classics Project (CSCP) and had been a main reason behind the setting up of the Cambridge Online Latin Project (COLP) in 1999: there was clear evidence in the late 1990s (see chapter 7) of an increasing shortage of classics teachers, particularly in maintained schools. At the same time there was, to judge by informal contacts with schools, growing interest in the possibility of introducing Latin as an enrichment course for able pupils in the early years of secondary school. This was the climate in which CSCP had set up COLP in 1999, nine months before the DfEE announced its intention to set up the KS3 pilot. In this chapter we follow the progress of one group of learners who took part in the initial COLP trial in 1999–2000. They started out in Year 8 as part of a larger group of twenty-five pupils learning Latin with an online tutor and ended up on the GCSE course being taught by a mixture of video-conference and traditional classroom teaching. While the experiences of this group of learners might not seem of direct relevance to many classics teachers, it is possible that at least some of the distance-teaching approaches used on the COLP pilot will be adopted by classroom teachers to supplement their traditional teaching, as the educational system changes to meet the needs and expectations of the digital age. This is certainly the hope of some educationalists:

> [the] traditional 'educational system' must be replaced by *polymorphic* educational provision – an infinite variety of multiple forms of teaching and learning. Future generations will look back on our current sharp disjunction between life and

---

[1] See pages 105–6 for information on the DfEE KS3 pilot.

education and our confusion of education with schools as a barrier blocking a – perhaps the – road to the learning society.

(Hargreaves 1997: 11; cited by Pachler 2001: 16)

The online Latin programme set up by CSCP marked a significant addition to the range of courses in classical languages available to independent learners. Unlike Open University courses it was specifically designed for school-aged pupils rather than mature students; unlike a language summer school its aim was not to provide a short, sharp burst of intensive teaching but a regular, sustained programme (which, since September 2006, goes through to GCSE). And unlike summer schools it was aimed at Key Stage 3 and 4 pupils rather than sixth-formers and university undergraduates. The only comparable course was the Rowley Regis Latin Summer School (now the Sandwell Latin Summer School) – though the term 'summer school' is misleading, since the six days of the summer school represent a very small proportion of the teaching programme offered by the Sandwell team and provide only a taster for the weekly classes that take place throughout the following two years and culminate in the GCSE examination. A key aspect of the Sandwell Latin Summer School is that, as a local non-residential summer school operating within the school term, it can work with younger students than those who normally attend residential summer schools. These students therefore have the chance to take GCSE Latin alongside their other GCSEs at the end of Year 11. This is a long-standing and highly successful scheme and, given the challenging nature of the local area (the most recent Ofsted report (2002) described Sandwell as 'characterised by a falling population and worsening relative levels of deprivation ... it is the most deprived borough in the West Midlands and there are no significant areas of affluence within its boundaries'), the fact that more than twenty pupils every year are taking GCSE Latin through the Sandwell Latin Summer School represents a major achievement.

Apart from the quality and commitment of the teachers and the leadership of Myles Walker, who has run the programme since 1978, the key to the success of the Sandwell Latin Summer School lies in the support provided centrally by Rowley Regis College and, since its closure, the local authority (LA), and in the strong links between Myles Walker and the liaison teachers in the individual schools who play an important role in recruiting pupils, identifying those likely to benefit from and enjoy the summer school and encouraging them to enrol. As part of its 14–19 Learning Programme Sandwell LA is committed to protecting minority subjects, and finances not only the summer school but also the peripatetic teachers who teach an hour a week off-timetable in all the schools with pupils taking Latin to GCSE.

The Sandwell Latin Summer School offers a robust and effective model of outreach for LAs in urban areas where there is a high concentration of classics teachers from independent schools in a position to teach on the summer school and two or three peripatetic teachers willing to work in five or six different schools every week. But its dependence on funding from the LA and a reliable supply of classics teachers makes it an impractical model for providing access to Latin nationally. With the CSCP online courses, on the other hand, the geographical location of the teacher ceases to be relevant, and CSCP itself can provide the infrastructure, if not the funding, provided by the LA, and can also help ensure consistency and quality of teaching through its training programme for online teachers (hereafter referred to as e-tutors). In other respects there are distinct similarities between the CSCP online Latin programme and the Sandwell Latin Summer School: the primary target group is Key Stage 3 pupils (though there is also an independent learner's course open to students of all ages); it depends on close liaison between the e-tutor and link teacher in school (hereafter referred to as facilitator); and it is based on weekly teaching sessions that run throughout the academic year (overseen by the facilitator following the scheme of work set by the e-tutor).

COLP year 1, 1999–2000

The origins of COLP lay in a Latin class of six Year 6 pupils from two local primary schools in north Essex whom I taught out of school hours in the mid-1990s. In conversation with the children's parents it emerged that attempts had been made to persuade the local comprehensive (School C)[2] to introduce Latin as an option in Key Stage 3, but without success. Nevertheless, in January 1999 I wrote to the deputy head at the school, a modern linguist known to be sympathetic to Latin, and to the headteacher of another local comprehensive (School D),[3] a colleague in the 1980s who had approached me informally about the possibility of starting up Latin, to see if they were interested in taking part in a pilot project to investigate the learning benefits of an online Latin programme. Both schools gave a very positive response: School C was already

---

[2] School C is a mixed comprehensive of approximately 2,000 pupils in a semi-rural area. It is a specialist technology college and a DfES-accredited training school. In its most recent Ofsted report (2003) it was described as 'a very good school with many excellent features'.
[3] School D is a mixed Roman Catholic comprehensive of approximately 900 pupils in an urban area. It was given performing arts college status in 2003. Ofsted described it as 'a very good school' in its most recent report (2004).

exploring ways of using the internet as part of a collaboration with a school in south London with whom it hoped to form a 'virtual' Education Action Zone[4] and was also looking for ways to address a dip in performance among Year 8 pupils, which had been identified in an internal school review; School D was particularly interested in finding ways to stretch able pupils and develop pupils' independent learning skills. By the end of May 1999 the Cambridge Faculty of Classics had given £3,650 towards general set-up costs and the Faculty of Education Research Development fund had committed £4,450 towards the monitoring and evaluation of the pilot. Meanwhile, the schools each appointed a member of staff to take overall responsibility for the Latin cohort and also to act as researcher; and although COLP was initially set up only as a one-year pilot, the schools nevertheless gave an undertaking to give the pupils the option to carry on with the Latin to GCSE if there was sufficient interest, finances permitting.

COLP was formally launched in the Museum of Classical Archaeology in Cambridge on 29 September 1999 with a lunch for the forty-five pupils (twenty-five Year 8 pupils from School C and twenty Year 9 pupils from School D) who had been selected for the pilot – chosen on the basis of cognitive attainment tests in School C and by performance in modern foreign languages in School D – and the nine PGCE trainees who were going to act as their e-mail tutors. After an introduction to the Cambridge Latin Course (CLC) given to the group as a whole, the pupils had a half-hour session with their e-tutor, each of whom was assigned a group of five pupils, for whom they set work on a weekly basis, tailored to the needs of the individual pupils, and provided feedback on their written work as and when appropriate. At the beginning of October both Latin classes were given a further one-hour lesson, taking them through Stage 1 of CLC Book I. Thereafter the pupils met once a week in their respective schools for a study session of approximately fifty minutes: in School C the class met after school, sometimes in a computer suite and sometimes in a classroom equipped with three computers, supervised by the COLP researcher, who was an experienced modern languages teacher; and in School D the class was run in lunchtimes in a computer suite, overseen by the headteacher himself.

Pupils worked through the CLC at their own pace, mostly in small groups but occasionally on their own, in an atmosphere that

---

[4] Education Action Zones were one of a range of policy initiatives set up in the late 1990s to improve standards through collaboration between schools. School C and its partner school set up their 'virtual' Education Action Zone in 2000.

was less formal than a normal lesson but more formal than a club. The pilot course ran for the autumn and spring terms and lasted twenty-four weeks, by the end of which everyone had reached the end of Stage 4 (out of twelve) of CLC Book I and a few were on Stage 8. The end of the pilot was marked with a visit to the Bay of Naples. Twenty of the twenty-five Year 8 pupils from School C chose to continue with Latin in Year 9; but pupils in School D were not offered the option of continuing, as it was felt unrealistic to expect pupils to reach GCSE in two years. But both schools went on the following year to take part in the DfEE KS3 pilot, to which they made a significant contribution in terms of the structure and organisation of the service to schools with no Latin teacher: the teacher-researchers not only drafted the guidelines for facilitators but also gave presentations at training days outlining the benefits of offering Latin and spelling out in detail the practicalities of setting up an online Latin course.

Lessons from the first year: communication

The initial aim of the COLP pilot, in terms of research, had been to examine the perceived benefits for able pupils of a distance-learning Latin programme, but it soon became clear that other, more practical, issues needed to be addressed before any meaningful research could be conducted into learning gains – in simple terms, there were such significant problems with the ICT element of the project that there were insufficient data to draw any conclusions about learning gains for the pupils. Three aspects of the ICT caused particular problems in the first term. Firstly, all twenty pupils in School D were given a single e-mail address to share (this was solved relatively quickly). Secondly, a number of the e-tutors had limited experience of e-mail. This was more difficult to address, and even after the trainees concerned had learnt the basics of e-mailing there remained a significant gap in expertise across the nine trainees, which directly affected their performance as e-tutors. But the most intractable problem was the lack of reliable internet access and other shortcomings in School C's ICT provision. The fact that the computer suite was unable to cope with twenty-five pupils logging on to the system at the same time was particularly disappointing given that the school was a specialist technology college. This undermined the facilitator's and the pupils' confidence in the technology and seriously affected pupils' ability to communicate with their e-tutor. Only pupils with internet access at home could keep in regular contact; pupils who missed the session and did not have internet access at home, could, and did, lose touch with their e-tutor for weeks at a time. There were also considerable differences in the extent to which the e-tutors had access to the internet or, rather, in the regularity with which they checked their e-mail account[5] (from three or four times a day to once every three or four days). The resulting infrequency of communication clearly restricted the pupils' and e-tutors' ability to get to know each other (in so far as that is possible via e-mail) and led to a loss of momentum and motivation on both sides.

The use of e-mail as the primary means of communication affected the teaching and learning process in one or two important ways. Firstly, it limited e-tutors to setting written, i.e. typed, assignments, since the schools did not have the scanning facilities to send other types of work, such as drawings and diagrams, digitally;[6] and in fact, because of the unreliability of internet access, even work that pupils typed was sometimes sent to the e-tutors by standard mail. Secondly, many pupils found typing up their written assignments a slow and laborious process, so that when they did have access to a computer their time was taken up not with learning Latin but with the mundane task of typing. Thirdly, e-mail presented challenges for e-tutors as a medium for giving feedback and answering pupils' queries: how does one respond in an e-mail to the request from a Year 8 pupil in School C who wrote, 'I would also appreciate it if you could send me some work on the tenses as I often get confused and want to get it clear in my head!!!!!!'? What you want to do in this situation is sit down and talk to the pupil. As it was, attempts to have a sort of typed conversation failed: because of the sometimes lengthy gaps between e-mails (there was no facility for synchronous communication), e-mail correspondence could not generate the pace of exchange needed to take forward pupils' understanding, and when pupils experienced difficulties with their work, identifying and addressing their needs could be a protracted and frustrating process. As one pupil graphically described it, 'waiting weeks for a reply can be a bit like getting a lesson through a syphon'. This was an issue picked up by Rod Jackson during research into the role of e-tutors on the DfEE KS3 pilot:

> One key pedagogical issue that five e-tutors explicitly identified regarding teaching and learning asynchronously was the absence of the immediate response, the instant feedback, the on-the-spot diagnosis which is such an integral part of classroom teaching ...

---

[5] Of course the PGCE trainees had many other commitments apart from their responsibilities as e-tutors, and deserve great credit for the part they played in COLP.
[6] Nor could the schools send such assignments by fax, as the e-tutors had no access to a fax machine in Cambridge.

The nature of the asynchronous dialogue between e-tutor and student was also felt to be fundamentally and, perhaps, qualitatively different from the dialogue that takes place in a classroom. [One e-tutor commented]: 'I think from the point of view of the students, they can't get an immediate answer, can they? And then it's difficult to have a dialogue, it's one question and then it's my response, you can't have an extended dialogue.'

(Jackson 2005: 15)

Apart from e-mail, the other ICT component of the course was a website set up to provide electronic resources and activities, such as quizzes and a vocabulary tester, to supplement the textbook; and in order to encourage the pupils to use it, they were set an assignment to design a tourist guide to Pompeii, paper-based or digital, using the resources and links provided on the website. Even so, the website was not used a great deal by the pupils, mainly because of the limited access to the internet discussed above, but partly because, just as with the pupils in Tenley Laserson's research (see page 114), many of the pupils preferred to use the textbook as their main resource: even though it was the opportunity to work on computers that had originally attracted many of the pupils to the Latin project, in practice they spent most of their time in study sessions working from CLC Book I and the *Independent Learning Manual*. This reflected a generally traditional approach to their weekly Latin sessions: even when they had access to a computer suite, most pupils in both schools chose to spend most of their time working from their textbooks rather than on the computer.[7]

Nevertheless, the two schools felt that the use of technology had been an important element in the project, not because it assisted the pupils' understanding of Latin but because it changed pupils' perception of e-mail and the internet which, until their participation in the COLP pilot, they had associated primarily with out-of-school leisure activities rather than with education and learning. It helped them develop a mature understanding of e-mail as a means of communication and highlighted its potential value as a means of gaining access to specialist knowledge. Furthermore, regular guaranteed access to computing facilities as part of the COLP pilot remained a strong motivational factor for pupils with no access to computers at home, in spite of the manifest frustrations, and helped

---

[7] Burch, Hitscher and Wachter (2005: 7) report a similar attitude among students in Switzerland piloting *Latinum electronicum*, an online Latin course for university beginners: '61% of the students said that they had difficulties in motivating themselves to learn with *Latinum electronicum* and that they did not like to learn with computer programmes in general. This correlates well with the result that 25% of the students have worked exclusively with the textbook, 46% mainly with the textbook, and that only 25% have worked five hours or more a week with the computer.'

dispel any notion that Latin was an old-fashioned subject. It should also be noted that in both schools there were pupils who had the interest and expertise to take full advantage of the opportunities to use ICT in their work: one pupil's assignment on the tourist guide to Pompeii took the form of an informative and well-designed web page, which he added to his own existing website; another pupil acted as the COLP party's photographer on the visit to the Bay of Naples, taking dozens of photographs every day on his digital camera, which he then downloaded, edited and catalogued on a laptop every evening. These may be commonplace activities today, but in 2000 they were ground-breaking and a valuable demonstration of the way ICT could be integrated into Latin teaching.

Lessons from the first year: motivation and independent learning

Most of the forty-five pupils on the pilot were highly motivated learners who for the most part willingly gave up an hour a week of their free time to attend Latin classes. This was demonstrated by the fact that in School C twenty out of twenty-five pupils chose to continue with Latin into Year 9. But they continued in spite of, rather than because of, the extent to which they were expected to work independently. They were not used, for instance, to working at their own pace and being given responsibility for submitting work for marking as and when appropriate. They also found it disconcerting to have their work marked by a tutor whom they never saw: 'It's hard not having a tutor, because there's no one to discipline me', observed one pupil, who clearly did not think that the e-mail tutor counted as a tutor! Another commented, 'I'm finding the work quite difficult because we are working so individually'; and a third pupil said, 'I feel a bit nervous about learning Latin without a teacher because it's hard if I get stuck but now it's not too bad.'

Such comments indicate pupils' dependence on other people, fellow-pupils as well as teachers, to help sustain their motivation and overcome gaps in understanding – though the comment from the third pupil suggests that some pupils learnt in time to become more independent. In School C where, as part of the research, the teacher made a conscious effort to act only as a facilitator and made no attempt to direct or help with the pupils' work (this was seen as the responsibility of the e-tutor), it took time for the pupils to accept that a teacher whom they knew to be an excellent languages teacher was not in a position to help them with their work. For the teacher, too, it took time to adjust to this change in status. Conversely in School D, where the sessions were supervised by the headteacher, a mathematician whom the pupils did not expect to help them with their Latin, the headteacher admitted that he often found it impossible to stay in the role of facilitator and frequently, in the early stages, intervened if he saw pupils struggling with something he himself understood!

With the teacher in the classroom acting only as facilitator, not subject specialist, effective learning depended on pupils developing a strong relationship with their e-tutor. It was for this reason that time had been set aside at the formal launch of COLP for the e-tutors to have an initial brief session with their five pupils, but thereafter the extent to which pupils and e-tutors got to know each other and established a good working relationship depended heavily on their ability to convey their interests, and indeed personality, through their e-mail exchanges. As has already been seen, e-mail had significant limitations as a medium for generating the sort of dialogue needed to promote effective learning, but at a less formal level a number of the e-tutors found ways of establishing genuine contact with their pupils. The skill lay in finding the right tone for e-mail communication, combining the informality of conversation with the conventions of a letter, as in this example:[8]

> Dear all
>
> This goes against the grain – I hate chain letters as they're so impersonal – but time pressures mean that my chances of marking all your work and tailoring follow-up tonight are slim. To avoid you kicking your heels, here's a suggestion to keep you ticking over...
>
> Rumour has it that it's hoped we get to Stage Four (or beyond) by Christmas. It's not a race; of course it's not – but you'd certainly be doing fantastically to have got that far by then (especially seeing that we're wandering a little down the history too). So, how about getting your teeth into the new grammar point in Stage 4, which introduces two new forms of verb: I and YOU (singular). You'll notice something about all 'I' verbs in Latin and all 'YOU' verbs. In English, we use the words I and YOU (and HE/SHE, WE, etc.) to show who's in charge of the verb. In Latin they had words with similar meanings, but gave another clue too.

The e-tutor here cajoles rather than coerces: the indirect appeal to his group's competitive instincts ('It's not a race; of course it's not – but...'!) may increase the chances that they will look at the new grammar point, and his explanation of the new forms of the verb

---

[8] For a detailed discussion of the language of e-mail see Crystal (2001).

leaves them with something to look out for. In this way the e-tutor manages to provide motivation and challenge in the same way that a classroom teacher would. But overall the COLP pupils missed the reassuring nagging, prompting, encouraging, questioning and explaining of everyday lessons. As one pupil succinctly expressed it, 'I like being taught.' The lesson from the initial pilot was clear: while ICT could augment the teacher's classroom repertoire, it could not replace the teacher's expertise: the computer might be a very powerful tool for providing and accessing information, but was still a relatively blunt instrument for helping the independent learner, no matter how well motivated, to acquire knowledge and understanding.

COLP year 2: the bulletin board

Only one school continued into the second year of the COLP pilot. In School D the online Latin programme was run as a one-year enrichment course and continued to be run on that basis for the DfEE KS3 pilot in 2000–1. In School C, on the other hand, where the pupils had started Latin in Year 8, the aim from the outset had been to offer it through to GCSE provided there was sufficient interest and, as noted earlier (page 129), twenty of the twenty-five students on the pilot chose to continue with Latin in Year 9. With the PGCE trainees now in their first teaching posts, there was also a change in the e-tutoring arrangements. The five PGCE trainees who had tutored the twenty-five pupils in Year 8 were replaced in Year 9 by a single e-tutor, an experienced classics teacher. The teacher faced a challenging brief: the pupils had reached different points in the course; in Year 9 they shared their after-school Latin session with the new Year 8 cohort who were part of the DfEE KS3 pilot; and the pace at which they covered the CLC had to increase in order to ensure that the GCSE remained an attainable target.

Responding to feedback from pupils and discussion with the facilitator, the e-tutor provided a much tighter schedule of work for Year 9, and posted each week's tasks on a bulletin board (a web-based discussion area, allowing asynchronous contributions from all members of the bulletin board, which could be stored permanently for later reference). While this saved the e-tutor a great deal of time, because she no longer had to e-mail the pupils individually (though she could do so when she wanted a private word), and while the bulletin board provided a valuable public record of each week's tasks, it was nevertheless an unsatisfactory form of communication because it, like e-mail, was dependent on pupils, and the e-tutor, having frequent, reliable access to the internet. There was another problem with the bulletin board: it was open to abuse by pupils, one or two of whom began to post inappropriate messages, such as:

> i do not like homework. do not send it.

> u r gay.

The authors were immediately identifiable – no postings could be made without giving one's identity – and the matter soon dealt with. Furthermore, it was clear the pupils themselves were aware that such messages were unacceptable. No sooner had the second message above appeared on the web board than a further message was posted:

> These posts were not written by Stuart and I, and were obviously a joke. This goes for the 'I don't like homework' post, and we are trying to work out how to erase them. Please do not take offence, and I will send my homework mail soon... :)

Happily there were very few inappropriate messages, and in general the messages posted by pupils showed a mature and responsible attitude to their learning. For instance, one pupil who only contacted the e-tutor via the bulletin board for the first time weeks after the start of the autumn term, wrote:

> I am sorry that I haven't been in touch with you. I am keeping up quite well with the work that you have been setting. I am on the end of stage 9 and I am in the middle of working on 'in taberna' answering the questions in the exercise books that we have been given today. I will finish that over the half term and do practising the language and learn the vocab list. Would you like me to E-mail you the answers to 'in taberna'? Also, I wouldn't mind if I am set a bit more to do over the holidays, as I would like to finish book 1 as soon as possible. I will try to keep in better contact from now on, with both E-mail and the WebBoard.

Another pupil reached a decision relatively early in the year not to take Latin to GCSE but the decision was not accompanied by any loss of motivation or interest:

> I am on stage 9 and I am half way through 'in palaestra' at the moment. I am sorry to say I only completed half of the revision work you set. Would it be possible if you could you please tell me where you would like me to be at in the course and what stages by Christmas. I have enjoyed doing the course and am finding it a valuable experience, but I have decided that I would not like to study it for my GCSEs. This means that I am not in an immense rush to get onto book 2. Thank you very much.

By the end of the year, a small group had formed who worked together in the after-school sessions and were determined if possible to continue Latin in Year 10. Out of the twenty pupils who took Latin in Year 9, seven students elected to take GCSE Latin (joined later by a Year 9 student who had transferred from an independent school where she had already started Latin). Given the extent to which the pilot was charting new waters and given the difficulties experienced with internet access, it was very encouraging that more than one in four pupils chose to go on to the GCSE. While the e-tutors and facilitator played a very important role in supporting the pupils, this should be attributed above all to the commitment and enthusiasm of the pupils themselves.

COLP year 3: video-conferencing

When asked what had persuaded them to opt for GCSE Latin, the almost unanimous response from the Year 10 group was 'the promise of having a teacher'! ICT had been essential in providing the class with access to Latin in the first place, but the pupils were clear that it was no substitute for a teacher. Once the decision had been made to run Latin through to GCSE it was agreed that in order to complete the course by the end of Year 11 there would have to be a great deal of face-to-face teaching. Instead of a single after-school session, theoretically an hour long but in practice nearer forty minutes, in Years 10 and 11 there were two lessons a week before school, from 8.00 to 8.40, with no possibility of over-running as assembly was at 8.45. They had a change of teacher once again, and the mode of teaching also changed, from e-tutoring to video conference (VC) teaching, although the teacher continued to use the bulletin board for posting the week's work, including homework assignments, and the occasional web links. Homework was still submitted and marked by e-mail.

The decision to switch to VC teaching was prompted mainly by concerns about the inadequacies of e-mail communication as a medium for teaching concepts rather than providing information. The experience of the first two years of COLP suggested that the pupils would struggle to understand increasingly complex aspects of the language without the '*immediate* response, the *instant* feedback, the *on-the-spot* diagnosis which is such a part of classroom teaching' (emphasis added), as the e-tutor cited by Jackson (2005) expressed it. In addition, there remained considerable variations in the extent to which pupils had access to the internet: some could access the internet only at school; others had only occasional access to the family computer in competition with other family members, and one pupil who did not have her own e-mail account had to use her father's throughout the GCSE course; the three boys in the group, on the other hand, were permanently online at home, often till late in the night.

Year 10 began with traditional classroom teaching. This not only enabled the teacher to establish a relationship with the class and make an initial assessment of their capabilities, but also helped to create a sense of purpose and momentum. This was much needed since the slowest in the group had only reached CLC Book II Stage 15 by the end of Year 9. The first few sessions were spent consolidating their knowledge of key language structures and working at vocabulary. In spite of significant gaps in their knowledge – hardly surprising given that they had had only approximately fifty Latin sessions in two years – the class had many of the characteristics needed to succeed in the GCSE. They were inquisitive, interested in language, self-disciplined, highly motivated and totally committed to the subject; above all, their experiences on the first two years of the project had helped them become a mutually supportive and good-humoured group.

The first VC link-up did not take place until the third week of term, and then it was with the limited aim of familiarising the teacher and class with the VC equipment and sorting out any teething problems with the technology. With this in mind for the first session, the teacher joined the pupils in the sixth-form teaching room where the VC equipment had been installed, while a colleague from CSCP dialled in from Cambridge. As was to be expected, there were a number of problems: there was no technician available to help when the first attempts to link up failed; once the link was established, it took a considerable amount of time to set up the furniture so that all the pupils were in camera shot; and there was constant noise from a building site outside the VC suite at the Cambridge end. Technical problems with the link-up were soon solved, but other difficulties with setting up the VC sessions remained: because the VC suite was housed in a regular classroom, the furniture had to be arranged at the start of each session and put back again at the end, taking away valuable time from the lessons; no technician was available at 7.55 to switch on the VC equipment (in the end one of the pupils, overseen by the facilitator, took on this responsibility); and the major building works outside the window of the VC suite in Cambridge continued to disrupt sessions all year.

Then there were issues connected with teaching and learning in a VC environment. When asked for their thoughts on VC lessons six weeks into term, the pupils said that they felt awkward in front of the camera (this did not last long) and found it hard to speak loud enough to be heard clearly by the teacher (this took a little longer to get used to). They also picked up on more intractable problems caused by the indifferent picture and sound quality of the VC equipment. As Gill Mead, an experienced VC teacher, notes:

> with the current state of technology, [VC] is a very broad brush medium. The picture quality at present is such that one cannot pick up the nuances of facial expression, the glazing over of the eyes, the shift of position, the sudden avoidance of direct eye contact – all those tics and quirks to which the antennae of the classroom teacher are instinctively alive. One cannot pick up the clues that express understanding and misunderstanding.
>
> (Mead 2005: 4)

This was a particular problem when it came to class discussion: it was hard to generate purposeful dialogue with everyone in the class. 'Rules of engagement' had to be spelt out even more clearly than in the traditional classroom, and, given the absence of the teacher's controlling presence, the class had to be all the more self-disciplined in the observance of them. Even so these problems occasionally caused frustration (on both sides). However, Adrian Spooner argues that the very difficulties VC teaching presents make it successful:

> Every time you go on line, you'll be reminded of the problems. So you compensate. You redouble your listening and watching, you concentrate on your clarity of delivery and your use of body language and eye contact. You are driven to check understanding repeatedly and take the social and intellectual temperature. You make sure your enthusiasm is conveyed and picked up. Then you notice that the students are similarly straining every sinew in their work and responses.
>
> (Spooner 1999: 6)

Gill Mead also argues that the limitations of VC encourage good classroom practice:

> Students need clear instructions. They need to develop listening skills. They need to respect each other's right to speak without interruption. So the medium demands courtesy. It reinforces good classroom practice not just because listening, taking turns and not interrupting are nice and polite, but because without them the medium does not work. Also, the need to be measured and thoughtful encourages more measured and considered answers.
>
> (Mead 2005: 4–5)

Certainly the class preferred VC to electronic communication via the bulletin board and e-mail. They said that they liked 'having a teacher you can see, who structures the lessons and sets deadlines' – though perhaps they meant 'enforces' rather than 'sets' deadlines since there were plenty of deadlines on the bulletin board! They also appreciated the regular reinforcement of vocabulary and language structures from one lesson to the next. These advantages flowed, of course, from the synchronous nature of VC communication, which enabled the 'real time interaction' of the normal classroom. Even so the teacher–pupil relationship in the VC classroom was subtly different from that in a normal classroom:

> So what advantages does videoconference have in the distance learning of Latin? For the students, there is real time interaction with an obviously human Latin specialist, in a situation which mimics the normal classroom experience, perhaps mundanely so. The routine could be a snapshot of any ordinary Latin lesson in any ordinary classics classroom, the ordinary litany of commands and questions – open your books at page X, do exercise Q, etc.

> But to use videoconferencing as simply a teacher substitute is to ignore the peculiar features of the medium and the opportunities it offers for creative interaction. Let us look at relationships first. Just as the teacher–pupil relationship in Internet exchange is different from normal classroom practice, so this VC relationship is also subtly different. With many established groups, it is the pupils who set up the VC kit. They positively invite the teacher into the classroom by dint of switching on and dialling in; so there is a nuanced difference in relationship. They can control sound and picture quality; this is also part of the dynamic. They can also, potentially, switch off!! They therefore have to be willing and mature collaborators, not only in the technology but also in their own learning. This modified power relationship becomes even more amorphous when you imagine what it is like for a group of large, bright 16-year-olds to be listening to pearls of wisdom from an 18x18 screen! There are obvious constraints on classroom management; physical presence and movement can no longer be part of the battery of teacher skills.

> (Mead 2005: 3)

The VC lessons themselves were indeed in many ways very similar to a traditional lesson in structure as well as delivery. A typical lesson might, for instance, entail some vocabulary work as a warm-up, then a brief discussion of the most recent homework assignment followed by translation of the next story in the CLC, before closing with quick-fire consolidation of the new language feature for the stage. There were one or two significant differences, however: as Gill Mead says, 'reading and researching lessons, where the pupils read and the teacher looks on, are patently ridiculous' (Mead 2005: 3). In order to maximise the real-time interaction with the class, almost all sessions were devoted to whole-class teaching with little or no individual or paired work, and as a consequence the class did very little writing in the VC classes. This enforced shift to an exclusively oral approach had a number of benefits: it required the pupils to listen to and speak Latin every lesson; it gave them a strong sense of the narrative of the CLC Books II and III because of the pace at which they could read stories when not required to write down a translation; and pace also helped reinforcement of vocabulary. On the negative side, there was less opportunity to assess a pupil's individual progress in lessons because there was no VC equivalent to circulating round the classroom to carry out the constant monitoring that characterises effective formative assessment.[9] *All* communication was public: this directly affected the way encouragement and criticism could be expressed and made it potentially more difficult for pupils to voice concerns or ask questions – though private communication remained available via e-mail.

Gill Mead sees possible gains from the apparent disadvantages of this very public teaching:

> [The] necessarily grand, public approach means that teaching cannot be as finely nuanced as in the normal classroom. One cannot engage in discreet, private and one-to-one explanations, that boon for the timid or quietly puzzled. This is not necessarily a disadvantage. Just as the constraints of the technology foster a mature approach among the learners, this constraint too encourages an honest, accepting and supportive culture requiring an attentive and sympathetic community of learners. It requires learners to be assertive and honest about their problems and their peers to be accepting, non-judgmental partners in learning.
>
> (Mead 2005: 4)

It was certainly true that the class displayed many of the positive characteristics identified above (but then they had done so in Year 9, long before the VC teaching began), and the lack of one-to-one teaching was more an issue for the teacher than the pupils, because of the extent to which it limited opportunities for formative assessment of, and feedback to, individual pupils. It was for this

---

[9] Homework assignments of course provided ample opportunity to monitor written work.

reason that towards the end of Year 10 the VC sessions were interspersed with face-to-face teaching with increasing frequency.

COLP year 4: back to the classroom

By the beginning of Year 11 the class had reached CLC Book III, Stage 27, a long way behind schedule, particularly since there were other pressures, academic and social, the pupils were likely to face in Year 11. Six of the eight pupils were taking fast-track languages, which involved a third early morning session; half the class had jobs; and attendance had begun to be an issue with one pupil in particular. Taking into account mock examinations, there were fewer than thirty weeks to cover the GCSE specifications, and the decision was therefore made to switch from VC to traditional classroom teaching for the final year. It was not merely the shortage of time that prompted the decision – although it had been found difficult to generate fast-paced lessons in VC sessions – but also concerns about VC as a medium for teaching the set texts, perhaps the most challenging aspect of Latin GCSE. The literature needed to be taken at a quick enough pace to give students a sense of the work, but slowly enough to ensure close familiarity with the text. Above all there needed to be a great deal of open discussion – an aspect of teaching particularly affected by the indifferent picture and sound quality – to ensure that the pupils could have the chance to develop their personal response to the literature through articulating their own thoughts and listening to those of others.

The class did not embark on the set texts until early November. Pressure of time meant that once again writing in lessons was kept to an absolute minimum and as a time-saving measure the pupils were provided with translation of the texts (though they were left to make their own notes on style and content). The Latin text was projected onto the whiteboard, providing a central focus and enabling the teacher to mark up aspects of language, choice of vocabulary, complex word order, and other points of interest. In this way the class would cover 12–15 lines of text in an average lesson, with focused, animated and – compared with similar VC lessons – fast-paced discussion involving all members of the class. It nevertheless took until the middle of April to complete the verse and prose prescription, leaving only three weeks to work on language and tackle unseens and comprehension exercises. Most language work had been undertaken as and when they encountered unfamiliar structures in the course of reading the set texts, with occasional detailed examination of specific aspects of grammar (such as indirect statement). Similarly, vocabulary was learnt wherever possible in the context of the literature. The cultural background topics were covered in a single two-hour class in the May half term, using video clips from the CLC Book I E-Learning Resource as a starting point for discussion.

The pupils from School C who started out with PGCE trainees as their e-tutors in 1999 and took the GCSE examination in summer 2002 received approximately 150 hours of tuition in total. This was significantly less than they would have received if they had been in a maintained school with timetabled Latin (see pages 94–5), but given the level of their commitment and the fact that they were high-attaining pupils (three of the class subsequently went to Oxbridge) it is perhaps not surprising that they achieved very good GCSE results (2 A*, 3 A, 1 B, 1 C, 1 D). Even the D represented something of a triumph: the student concerned was a very able linguist – he scored a creditable 38 out of 60 on the comprehension and unseen in the GCSE – but he attended Latin sessions very infrequently, telling me in an e-mail at one stage that mornings were not his strong point.

The course had proved demanding for pupils and teachers alike but in terms of research it yielded valuable insights into the strengths and limitations of ICT-based approaches to distance learning in Latin. Although traditional teaching methods were employed at the end of the GCSE course, the use of ICT to link up e-tutors with pupils meeting once a week in off-timetable classes supervised by a facilitator proved an effective way of engaging learners and led to very respectable recruitment through to Year 10.[10] Nevertheless, perhaps the strongest message to emerge from the pilot was the value attached by pupils to classroom teaching and the difficulty of replicating that powerful learning environment through electronic media. Classics teachers have no need to fear that they are about to be replaced by the computer.

References

Burch, I., Hitscher, S. and Wachter, R. (2005). '*Latinum electronicum*: a playful online Latin course for university beginners'. Paper given at international meeting of Latin teachers, Cambridge UK, July 2005. Available for download from www.cambridge.org/latinconference05; last accessed 2 December 2006

Crystal, D. (2001). *Language and the Internet*. Cambridge: Cambridge University Press

---

[10] For discussion of the crucial role of facilitators and the importance of their relationship with the e-tutors in sustaining pupils' motivation see Lister and Seranis (2005).

DfEE (2000). *The Key Stage 3 Educational Service Pilot: Prospectus*. London: DfEE

Hargreaves, D. (1997). 'A road to the learning society', *School Leadership and Management* 17(1), pp. 9–21

Jackson, R. (2005). 'E-tutors' experiences of teaching Latin via the Internet on the Cambridge Online Latin Project'. Paper given at international meeting of Latin teachers, Cambridge UK, July 2005. Available for download from www.cambridge.org/latinconference05; last accessed 2 December 2006

Lister, B. and Seranis, P. (2005). 'Access to specialist knowledge through information and communications technology: a case study', in *Teacher Development* 9(1), pp. 97–114

Mead, G. (2005). 'Videoconferencing Latin'. Paper given at international meeting of Latin teachers, Cambridge UK, July 2005. Available for download from www.cambridge.org/latinconference05; last accessed 2 December 2006

Pachler, N. (2001). 'Connecting schools and pupils: to what end?', in Leask, M. (ed.), *Issues in Teaching Using ICT*, pp. 15–30. London: RoutledgeFalmer

Spooner, A. (1999). 'TELEDIDAXIS: a sophistic note on handling video conferencing', *JACT Review* 2(26), pp. 5–6

10 Re-evaluating the role of ICT in classics teaching

The evidence from the Cambridge Online Latin Project (COLP) presented in chapters 8 and 9 suggests that while information and communication technology (ICT) has a significant role to play in widening access to and enriching the teaching of Latin, it should be seen not as a replacement for traditional teaching resources such as textbooks or for teachers themselves, but as a powerful supplement requiring skilful mediation by teachers to ensure that it is effectively integrated into the wider pattern of pupils' learning. Others share the view that there is no prospect of computers replacing teachers:

> My experiences as a teacher and educator strongly suggest that the role of the teacher, despite pressures to change towards that of a facilitator and creator of didactically prepared web-based learning material, remains absolutely central in rendering the experiences and work of pupils with and at the computer coherent.
>
> (Pachler 2001: 17)

> In spite of some of the claims made by 'techno-fundamentalists' suggesting that computers would obviate the need for schools to exist as centres of learning, and that teachers unable to use the new technology would have to be 'culled' from the profession, many schools and classrooms do not function in ways radically different from those of the BT (before technology) era.
>
> (Haydn 2003: 12)

Since the early years of COLP and the DfEE KS3 pilot there have been substantial improvements in ICT provision in schools and an exponential growth in home use of computers: both these developments have implications for teachers in the classroom. This chapter looks at changing attitudes to, and expectations of, ICT in the last ten years, and then considers ways in which school and classroom practice from the BT era may have to change in the light of continuing developments.

ICT – rhetoric and reality

When computers – or 'microcomputers' as they were called at the time, to distinguish them from mainframe computers – began to be manufactured in a size suitable for the classroom and at a price that schools could afford, their arrival was greeted with enthusiasm but also prompted questions:

> About this time [1978], we, flushed with the enthusiasm generated by our recent purchase of a Sinclair ZX80 computer, were beginning, however hesitantly, to ask ourselves questions about what we could do in the classroom with what was for us still a new, almost magical, and certainly mysterious, piece of equipment.
>
> (Adams and Jones 1983: 1)

Nearly thirty years later policy-makers, educationalists, headteachers and classroom practitioners are still asking the same questions about the role of the computer in the classroom and education more generally. During that time advocates of ICT have made extravagant claims for computers and have had very high expectations of the power of new technologies to transform education. As recently as 2003, in the introduction to *Fulfilling the Potential: Transforming Teaching and Learning through ICT in Schools* Charles Clarke, the Secretary of State for Education at the time, gave a long list of the ways in which ICT could make a 'massive' contribution to educational reform:

- ICT can make a significant contribution to teaching and learning across all subjects and ages, inside and outside the curriculum;
- ICT can provide opportunities to engage and motivate children and young people and meet their individual learning needs;
- ICT can help link school and home by providing access to teaching and learning materials, and to assessment and attendance data, from home;
- ICT can enable schools to share information and good practice in networked learning communities;
- intelligent information management systems within schools can support school leadership;
- integrated curriculum and management information systems can help schools monitor individual pupils' progress for assessment for learning as well as for administrative purposes;

- and use of shared drives in schools to bank lesson plans and other resources can produce vast savings in time and effort for teachers.

(DfES 2003: 2–3)

These were bold claims, given the chequered success of previous ICT initiatives. Six years earlier the government's big idea had been the National Grid for Learning. In his foreword to the government's consultation paper, *Connecting the Learning Society*, Tony Blair set out his vision for ICT in education; in it he argued that technological change was the means 'to lift educational standards in Britain to the level of the best in the world' and put forward the National Grid for Learning as a key aspect in promoting effective use of ICT:

> Technology has revolutionised the way we work and is now set to transform education. Children cannot be effective in tomorrow's world if they are trained in yesterday's skills. Nor should teachers be denied the tools that other professionals take for granted.
>
> ... The Grid will be a way of finding and using on-line learning and teaching materials. It will help users to find their way around the wealth of content available over the Internet. It will be a resource for everyone in our schools. For example, a teacher will be able to get advice on effective ways of teaching children how to read. Pupils will be able to revise for their GCSEs or explore the museums of the world for their project work. Standards, literacy, numeracy, subject knowledge – all will be enhanced by the Grid.

(DfEE 1997: 1)

Both *Fulfilling the Potential: Transforming Teaching and Learning through ICT in Schools* and *Connecting the Learning Society* were much more concerned with enhancing access to information, mostly by teachers and administrators, than improving pupils' learning. The underlying assumption seemed to be that easier access to information would of itself enhance the learning process. This has been challenged by history specialists, among others: discussing the challenge facing teachers in the information-rich classroom of the internet-connected school, Terry Haydn argues that some pupils are confused enough by the existing quantity of facts they have to handle, without being confronted by a further limitless mass of information. What pupils need, he suggests, are skills to cope with the massive increase in the amount of historical information available, skills such as 'sifting and selecting, organising and classifying, prioritising and discarding, synthesising and marshalling information' (Haydn 2003: 19).[1] Susan Greenfield raised a connected issue in a newspaper article, comparing the internet unfavourably with the book as a means to 'turn information into knowledge':

> When you read a book, the author usually takes you by the hand and you travel from the beginning to the middle to the end in a continuous narrative of interconnected steps. It may not be a journey with which you agree, or one that you enjoy, but none the less, as you turn the pages, one train of thought succeeds the last in a logical fashion. We can then compare one narrative with another and, in so doing, start to build up a conceptual framework that enables us to evaluate further journeys, which, in turn, will influence our individualised framework. We can place an isolated fact in a context that gives it a significance. So traditional education has enabled us to turn information into knowledge.

> ... Navigation on the internet is wonderful – if you have a conceptual framework in which to embed the responses that flash up. But we should not assume that all children will be so well equipped.

> (Greenfield 2006)

A further assumption behind *Connecting the Learning Society* is that electronic resources are of themselves motivational ('Pupils will be able to revise for their GCSEs...'). But as computers and associated hardware increasingly become the main source of young people's leisure and entertainment (with games, films, music and communication with friends all available from a single hub) why should the fact that GCSE revision materials are available in electronic format on the internet mean that pupils will actually go and visit the relevant website? Evidence from a small-scale study[2] of pupils in three schools learning Latin online, in line with other research (for example, Deaney, Ruthven and Hennessy 2003; cited by Laserson 2005), suggests that computer-based study can quickly lose its novelty value and become as tedious and repetitive as the aspects of traditional study which it sought to replace. This issue was also picked by Ofsted in a recent report on ICT and the teaching of English:

> The use of ICT remains a motivating factor for many pupils in English; however, teachers need to understand that a badly behaved class does not improve merely by being seated in front

---

[1] These aims are addressed in the National Curriculum for ICT in so far as it requires that pupils at Key Stage 3 are taught 'to be systematic in considering the information they need and to discuss how it will be used' and 'how to obtain information well matched to purpose by selecting appropriate sources, using and refining search methods and questioning the plausibility and value of the information found' (DfEE/QCA 1999: 20)
[2] See Laserson 2005.

of computers. Some ICT tasks in English remain limited and fail to extend pupils' learning. Sometimes pupils spend time simply reading material on screen which would be better accessed from the printed page.

(Ofsted 2004a: 7)

A decade on from the publication of *Connecting the Learning Society*, on 13 April 2006, the National Grid for Learning was shut down – a victim of the unrelenting pace of change in the world of ICT which has made it so difficult to develop informed strategies for translating technological advances into improved classroom practice. In the mid 1990s, for instance, data projectors were so rarely found in schools that they were not even included in the government annual statistics on ICT provision in schools, but are now to be found in 99 per cent of schools and are increasingly used as the preferred medium for incorporating ICT in whole-class teaching; and increased use of data projectors has in turn fuelled demand for interactive whiteboards. What are the implications of these developments for teachers in the classroom? In what ways can the use of an interactive whiteboard contribute to the classics teacher's repertoire of strategies for teaching language or literature? These are the sorts of issues teachers should be considering, but faced with initiative overload and routine commitments (such as organising a school visit, marking coursework, preparing materials for a new GCSE course) they have very little time to develop their own computer skills, let alone investigate ways of integrating ICT into their own teaching.

This is one of a number of reasons why ICT has not as yet had the transformational effect on education hoped for by policy-makers and politicians. In *ICT in Schools: the Impact of Government Initiatives Five Years On*, published in 2004, Ofsted found that although 'the combined impact of government initiatives for ICT in schools has been significant', with dramatic improvements in teachers' competence in ICT and schools' ICT resources at record levels, at the same time:

The spread of ICT as a tool for teaching and learning has continued at a slow, albeit steady, rate. This is especially the case in secondary schools, where departmental organisation can hinder whole-school progress. As yet, the government's aim for ICT to become embedded in the work of schools is a reality in only a small minority of schools. More typical is a picture in which pupils' ICT experiences across the curriculum are sporadic and dependent on teachers; in many schools, opportunities to exploit the technology are lost on a daily basis.

(Ofsted 2004b: 6)

Why has the spread of ICT as a tool for teaching and learning been so slow? As the report indicates, it is certainly not for want of investment: since 1998 the government has put substantial sums of money into ICT in schools (£510 million in 2002–3 alone) and the training of teachers (Ofsted 2004b: 3). A survey of ICT in schools (DfES/Becta (The British Educational Communications and Technology Agency) 2004) showed that the ratio of pupils to computers in secondary schools in 2004 was 4.9:1 (compared with 8.7:1 in 1998); that, as mentioned above, 99 per cent had data projectors (up from 82 per cent in 2002), with an average of 12.8 per school; that 92 per cent of secondary schools had interactive whiteboards (up from 65 per cent in 2002), with an average of 7.5 per school; and that the overall expenditure on ICT was £91 per pupil (compared with £46 in 1998). The survey also showed that access to the internet and to e-mail had improved significantly: 84 per cent of schools provided all teaching staff with individual accounts and 60 per cent provided pupils with either an individual or a shared account.

ICT in the home

Nor can the limited impact of ICT on teaching and learning be attributed to a lack of relevant skills among pupils who now have far more opportunities, from a much younger age, to develop their skills than in the past. The biggest change in ICT in the last ten years has been the exponential growth of computers in the home: many children now have access to computers at home of a far higher specification than those they use in school and use them for extended periods of time, and for a wide range of activities, as table 7 shows.

Table 7   *Activities undertaken on the computer at home by 11- to 18-year-olds, autumn 2002*

Activity	Percentage
School/college work	90
Playing games	70
Using the Internet	67
Playing CDs	48
Using e-mail	45
Using CD-ROMs	42
Typing letters	33
Visiting chat rooms	17

Source: Office for National Statistics, retrieved from http://www.statistics.gov.uk on 3 August 2006.

This is a continuing trend: as more young people gain unrestricted access to a computer in the home, a similar survey would undoubtedly show a significant increase in the use of the computer for leisure activities. Not long ago there was generally a single computer in the house, located in a common area such as the sitting room where use of the computer could be closely monitored, but now many children are free to use their computer uninterrupted and unchallenged in the privacy of their own room. Furthermore, the power and speed of modern computers gives them access to a whole new world of creativity and experiment: they can now create their own music, edit photographs and videos, and put together multimedia presentations, all on the same machine. Whatever they create can then be 'published' instantly on the web. With broadband now widely available,[3] many children also have unrestricted access to the internet; once they log on in the evenings they can keep in constant contact with their friends through MSN Messenger, while checking out websites for their homework assignments, and downloading music to listen to on their MP3 players. Unlimited internet access also opens up the world of MMORPGs (massively multiplayer online role-playing games) such as *World of Warcraft*, which, by March 2006, had 6.5 million active subscribers worldwide, with more than half a million users online at any one time. Through sheer frequency of use young people soon acquire basic keyboard skills (even if most do not learn to touch-type) and are familiar with standard software packages long before they leave primary school. They have no fear of computers and are not put off by new developments in the technology: for instance, faced with an unfamiliar piece of software, by a process of informed guesswork based on their knowledge and expertise of existing software, they can usually master the basics of a new program in minutes. While clearly not all young people fit this description of the permanently online, multi-tasking, creative technophile – there are still children who prefer books to websites or kicking a football in the park to playing FIFA Street 2 on their Xbox – we should still assume that for the average secondary school pupil the computer is as much an integral part of their life as trainers or television.

ICT in the classroom

Given pupils' increased familiarity and confidence with computers, and given the improved access in schools to fast and reliable hardware, teachers are now in a better position than ever before to make effective

---

[3] In a survey in spring 2005 of forty-seven pupils learning Latin through the Cambridge Online Latin Project, Tenley Laserson (2005) found that all pupils had access to a computer at home, and all but one had internet access, twenty-nine of them using a broadband connection.

use of technology in their classrooms. So what has inhibited the embedding of ICT in classroom teaching? Ofsted identified two factors: first, continuing difficulties of access to computers for individual departments in spite of the improving pupil:computer ratio in secondary schools; and secondly, shortcomings in ICT training for teachers, in particular the training programme funded by the National Opportunities Fund in the late 1990s, concerning which Ofsted found that 'expected outcomes were not met in about a third of schools and were met significantly in only another third' (Ofsted 2004b: 4). Certainly classicists, and humanities teachers more generally, have often in the past found computer facilities monopolised by departments such as Technology and Business Studies; and ICT training for classicists has been very patchy.

But there are two further reasons for teachers making limited use of ICT in their teaching: firstly, until relatively recently there has been a lack of high-quality subject-specific software and digital teaching resources specifically designed for use in the classroom (as opposed to electronic resources for reference and research); and secondly, teachers – and, perhaps more important, pupils – have yet to be convinced that ICT, for all its potential as an information tool, is necessarily an effective teaching and learning tool. This was evident in the views of pupils on the COLP pilot (see pages 126–31): although they enjoyed using ICT resources to learn Latin, they were also aware of the limitations of electronic communication and electronic resources when it came to explaining concepts, providing feedback and sustaining motivation. Similar views have been expressed by pupils in other studies:

> Pupils were apprehensive about what they saw – actually and potentially – as a diminishing contribution of teachers to their activity. Currently, the more individualised patterns of activity in lessons conducted in ICT classrooms meant that pupils had relatively little interaction with the teacher, and that support was often not as readily available as they wished ... Potentially, pupils imagined teachers becoming still further removed, in a future where pupils would work independently at home. This led pupils to assert the importance of social facilitation in learning, particularly the role of teachers in regulating, structuring and supporting academic work, and the distinctively human qualities and personalising capacities that they brought to such tasks.
>
> (Deaney, Ruthven and Hennessy 2003: 160)

As recently as 2000 an article in *The Sunday Times*, 'Elite teachers to give lessons by computer', described a vision of an ICT-driven education system in which many teachers would be replaced by computers:

In the longer run, ministers envisage the computer lesson spreading to every school and subject, forging a new era of education characterised by:

- Class sizes of 70, with each pupil working exclusively on their own desk-top computer.

- These larger classes being instructed only by the best teachers, who will be paid more than the £23,500 maximum currently available to all but a few qualified 'superteachers'.

- Some of the new computer-age classes being on split sites, enabling minority subjects such as Latin – unavailable in some state schools – to be taught to small groups across the education authority's area by a single online teacher.

- Private schools agreeing to teach state school pupils. Latin students at inner-city schools could be instructed by an Eton master, whose own pupils are staring at the same computer instructions and questions.

(The Sunday Times, 9 January 2000)

Few would now argue that computers will replace teachers. Although it is possible to find examples of small groups being taught Latin across a local authority with a single online teacher, this is only happening where there are no classics teachers and where, without online provision, Latin would not be available at all. But the other three features of the 'new era of education' remain unfulfilled and would no longer be regarded by most people – including, as we have seen above, pupils – as desirable goals. Although there are *some* teaching functions that the computer can fulfil, its role is seen much more now as one that complements rather than replaces the teacher (Pisapia 1994). Few teachers would dispute that computers can make a positive contribution to classroom teaching, particularly now that computers are faster, more reliable and more readily available in school. We know, for instance, ways in which computers have the advantage over traditional tools: they are faster for certain tasks (e.g. looking up words), can enliven routine activities (e.g. vocabulary testing), and improve the presentation of pupils' work. Furthermore, in spite of the very uneven provision in ICT training, many teachers today have good computing skills – often acquired through hours working at the computer at home in the evenings. Many classicists are now ICT-literate and are sufficiently familiar with standard software packages to search the web for resources and word-process worksheets (perhaps incorporating graphics) and put together PowerPoint presentations.

Certainly, in terms of their attitude to ICT, classicists have come a long way since 1994 when a statistical survey by the Department for

Education found that only 20 per cent of classics teachers regularly used a computer and that, in the perception of headteachers, no classics teachers made 'substantial' use of computers in their teaching, 8 per cent made some use and 92 per cent made none (the corresponding figures for English teachers were 28, 69 and 3 per cent). At the time I wrote in the *JACT Review* that:

> The steady growth of information technology (IT) over the last ten years has not been welcomed by Classics teachers in secondary schools with unreserved enthusiasm. Some classicists barely acknowledge the existence of computers, and take pride in not knowing how to switch one on. Others, while conceding that computers may have their use in subjects such as Mathematics or Science, can see no benefit in having pupils use them in Classics lessons. Others again, while happy to use computers, resent the part that IT has played in the fierce struggle for space on the timetable, which has left many Classics departments having to accept a reduction in their lesson allocation, especially at Key Stage 3.

(Lister 1994: 20)

Classics teachers also have many more opportunities to use ICT in the classroom than a decade ago. Since the year 2000 there has been a dramatic increase, as we saw earlier (page 146), in the number of data projectors and interactive whiteboards in classrooms. These, when used in conjunction with a computer and speakers, provide the combined functionality of a slide projector, tape-recorder, video-recorder, CD player and DVD player, making it possible for the teacher to integrate a wide range of different resources seamlessly into a lesson. And if the classroom computer has an internet connection, teachers can also share the limitless resources of the world wide web with the class: when teaching Virgil *Aeneid* II, for instance, they can call up Lewis and Short online,[4] show pupils how to pronounce the Latin correctly,[5] or take them on a virtual tour of Troy.[6]

Blended learning
But although improvements in, and increased access to, ICT hardware have led to increased use of ICT in the classroom, it has not brought about the sort of transformation of teaching envisaged by some:

---

[4] Lewis and Short first published their Latin dictionary in 1879 and it is now available in electronic form on the Perseus Project site at http://www.perseus.tufts.edu (last accessed 2 December 2006).
[5] Read it Right! is available at http://www.classicsnet.plus.com/readitright.htm (last accessed 2 December 2006).
[6] Visit http://www.stoa.org/metis for virtual tours of main archaeological sites in Greece (last accessed 2 December 2006).

Advocates insist that technology can help transform curriculum, teachers' roles and even school structure. The teacher's role is to facilitate learning rather than lecture. Students use the potential of technology to communicate, access information, learn collaboratively, think critically and take initiative in planning and implementing curricular products.

(Pisapia 1994: 1)

The introduction of ICT has not as yet seen a significant shift towards more collaborative classrooms where the teacher's role is more that of a facilitator than director. Instead, much of the time ICT is being used to do old things in new ways rather than 'to make new things possible in new ways' (Noss and Pachler 1999: 196):

As each new technological innovation (radio, television, video etc.) has come and gone, it has left education with a feeling that something good has happened but that nothing fundamental has changed. Only a couple of years ago, hypertext and multimedia were thought to be the panacea of educational change. Yet all that has happened so far has been the translation into hypermedia of the pedagogical approaches which characterize technologies of a previous era.

William Magrath, Professor of Classics at Ball State University Indiana, illustrates the use of new technology to implement technologies of a previous era in his description of the students' view of a typical college lecture:

The eye travels the distance to the front and seeks out the professor. He is but a shadow in the presence of 'The Screen'. Eight feet wide by 10 feet tall, glittering with color, graphics, video segments, fades and reveals, the screen captures the eye. Its surface is bathed in multicolored, multifont text and clever images by the same digital projector from which emanate strains of melodies and small snatches of recitation. And, weaving it all together is the disembodied voice of the instructor.

(Magrath 2001: 283–4)

For Magrath, this type of multimedia presentation typifies Stage Two of the changing use of ICT in education,[7] which he calls 'static innovation'. What concerns him about this phase – in which 'PowerPoint presentations and Web pages rapidly replace the blackboard-cum-overhead-cum slide projector-cum VCR-cum-CD player' (Magrath 2001: 284) – is that this use of ICT tends to inhibit,

---

[7] Stage One, 'outside innovation', was marked by the use of e-mail and the Web for assignments.

rather than promote, interactive learning:

> With lights dimmed (for better projection), key points highlighted (for easier note taking), and delivery more like television as a medium (students become viewers), interactivity is at times no more than an empty slogan.
>
> (Magrath 2001: 284)

Magrath argues for a move away from uses of ICT that reinforce passive learning towards those that free up time in lectures for more active and collaborative learning: this is what he sees as the goal of Stage Three, 'dynamic innovation'. In the case of his own course on world mythology, this has involved transferring much of the course content and assessment from the lecture hall to the web, thereby enabling him to develop a different kind of dialogue with his students:

> much of my talking now can be at a different level since the students have already 'mastered' what I am talking about ... I can present and analyze, or present for analysis, more complicated examples of the issues under discussion ... I can create small groups, clustered in the fixed seating, to apply a theory and report findings without worrying about whether I have covered enough material in class for them to understand the task ... More informed and focused discussions can ensue.
>
> (Magrath 2001: 287)

One could argue that Magrath has merely provided his students with an online course schedule and pre-session reading, and that their use of ICT remains passive, but the fact that the materials are web-based (with extensive links to other sources) gives the students a sense of control: they can access the materials when and where they want to and can follow up links at their own leisure. Magrath also makes considerable use of ICT to extend his contact with students beyond the lecture hall:

> On a given day, I write comments on a student's first draft left in my electronic mailbox; I join a discussion on a bulletin board about whether family values are stronger in our society than in Greek myths; I respond to several student e-mails concerned about their grades in a recent quiz; I sign off on the outline of a small group project; I send out congratulations to those who have done very well in their essay...
>
> (Magrath 2001: 291)

The approach adopted by Magrath is generally known as 'blended learning', and is seen by some as the best way to integrate ICT into teaching and learning. For instance, a recent report from Canada argued that 'the most effective approach to educational technology adoption and use is to create rich mediated learning environments that employ a blend of interactive and non-interactive, synchronous and asynchronous, independent and collaborative learning technologies' (Alberta Education 2006: 92). Blended learning has its origins in distance learning programmes for adults and may seem, at first sight, to be of little relevance to classics teachers in secondary schools. But as the percentage of homes connected to the internet has increased, so has interest in exploiting the internet as a way to extend learning beyond the confines of the school. Becta has reported a rapid development of the technical infrastructure to support learning beyond school:

> There is increasing use of intranets, home-school email links, managed and virtual learning environments, handheld devices and podcasting. These represent indicators of progress towards access and availability of learning opportunities beyond the institution.
>
> (Becta 2006: 33)

Many classics teachers may need to consider incorporating elements of blended learning into their schemes of work, as a way of increasing the amount of time for teaching Latin up to GCSE. It may be necessary, for instance, to transfer some aspects of their teaching from the classroom to the web (for example, vocabulary tests and language reinforcement exercises) in order to maximise contact time for those aspects of the course that require whole-class interactive teaching (for instance, explaining grammar points and reading the set texts), and for teachers who use the Cambridge Latin Course (CLC) the CSCP website already provides a wide range of electronic materials that their pupils can access from home; and the *Book I E-Learning Resource* provides three different pathways through the CLC, drawing on both printed and electronic materials, which could be adapted to meet a school's individual needs.

Classics and National Curriculum ICT

At the time of writing it is unclear whether blended learning will find widespread acceptance in schools. Even classics departments that can see advantages in adopting some form of blended learning may be put off by the very heavy investment of time needed to set up such courses. A practical problem with blended learning is its dependence on the learner having home access to the internet; and there is evidence that teachers are deterred from setting homework explicitly requiring the use of ICT because of concerns about the digital divide in children's access to technology out of school (Valentine, Marsh and Pattie 2005; cited in Becta 2006).

There are other, less ambitious, ways of integrating ICT into classroom teaching, which make it possible for teachers to address both classics-specific and ICT objectives at the same time. A good example can be found in Ruthven, Hennessy and Deaney (2005), in which the authors evaluate five school projects exploring the incorporation of ICT into classroom teaching; amongst these was a project undertaken by a Latin teacher who, within a series of three lessons on preparatory research for GCSE coursework, wanted to develop strategies for helping students become 'independent, effective, efficient and discerning electronic information gatherers rather [than] remain as serendipitous and credulous surfer-browsers' (Ruthven, Hennessy and Deaney 2005: 22). While helping her pupils investigate their chosen coursework topic she was also addressing the NC learning objectives for ICT at Key Stage 4, which require that pupils are taught

   a how to analyse the requirements of tasks, taking into account the information they need and the ways they will use it

   b to be discriminating in their use of information sources and ICT tools.

(DfEE/QCA 1999: 22)

In the first lesson the class was restricted to using resources from the library stock; in the second, the pupils used only materials from the internet; and in the third they were free to use either. By this simple division of lessons the teacher was able to contrast 'the accessibility and acceptability of the highly filtered material in the library with the diversity and unpredictability, vivacity and currency, but sometimes dubious validity, of internet material' (Ruthven, Hennessy and Deaney 2005: 23), and encourage pupils to think explicitly about the relative value of the library and the internet as sources of information:

> And they all said 'Oh, the Internet's obviously better' ... 'Why is it better?' 'Because there's so much more information on it.' But slowly they began to get through to see the advantages and disadvantages of both ... [and the need] to be much more ... critical and discerning in their use of sites than they are with the book stock.
>
> (Ruthven, Hennessy and Deaney 2005: 24)

The teacher also sought to take her pupils beyond the gathering of facts towards more critical engagement with the material by talking to pupils individually about sites they had located and how it related to their chosen coursework topic:

> If they just have a title, a topic – food, gladiators, religion – it

tends to be what I call a 'bung essay' in that they just bung down random facts, and they don't actually organise the facts towards an argument which is what they get marks for. And one of the best ways of making sure that they are getting the marks ... is a question in their head, a kind of exam-type question: 'How did the Romans use food to confirm status?'; something like that. And then they can marshal their facts and produce an argument.

(Ruthven, Hennessy and Deaney 2005: 23)

Here the teacher directly addresses the crucial issue of translating information into knowledge discussed at the beginning of this chapter (see pages 143–4): she gives the pupils the scaffolding they need to explore the relationship between the items of information they have collected and bring them together in a coherent argument. By approaching Latin coursework in this way she both improves the chances of her pupils performing well in the GCSE examination and promotes the development of key research skills so important in the sixth form and beyond; and, in terms of ICT objectives, she has achieved her aim of helping make her pupils more responsible and discriminating internet users, thereby contributing to their broader educational development:

> *Mature* use of the Internet is not just a question of being able to search efficiently to locate information, helpful though this skill is. It is also about helping pupils to develop the 'media literacy' which is an important facet of education for citizenship.

(Haydn 2003: 23)

Classicists who integrate ICT – and citizenship – into their teaching in this way, as well as exploiting the rich range of digital resources now available for use in the classroom, are making a small but significant contribution to the future survival of classics in schools.

References

Adams, A. and Jones, E. (1983). *Teaching Humanities in the Microelectronic Age*. Milton Keynes: Open University Press

Alberta Education (2006). *Video-conferencing Research: Community of Practice Research Report*. Retrieved from http://www.vcalberta.ca/research/ 20 August 2006

Becta (2006). *The Becta Review 2006: Evidence on the Progress of ICT in Education*. Coventry: Becta

Deaney, R. Ruthven, K. and Hennessy, S. (2003). 'Pupil perspectives on the contribution of information and communication technology to teaching and learning in the secondary school', *Research Papers in Education* 18(2), pp. 141–65

DfEE (1997). *Connecting the Learning Society*. London: DfEE

DfEE/QCA (1999). *The National Curriculum for England: Information and Communication Technology*. London: DfEE/QCA

DfES (2003). *Fulfilling the Potential: Transforming Teaching and Learning through ICT in Schools*. London: DfES

DfES/Becta (2004). *ICT in Schools Survey 2004*. London: HMSO

Greenfield, S. (2006). 'We are at risk of losing our imagination', *The Guardian*, 25 April 2006

Haydn, T. (2003). 'Computers and history: rhetoric, reality and the lessons of the past', in Haydn, T. and Counsell, C. (eds.), *History, ICT and Learning in the Secondary School*. London: RoutledgeFalmer

Laserson, T. (2005). 'To what extent can electronic resources enhance the study of Latin?' Unpublished MPhil thesis, University of Cambridge Faculty of Education

Lister, B. (1994). 'Classics and information technology in secondary schools', *JACT Review* 2(16), pp. 20–1.

Magrath, W. (2001). 'A return to interactivity: the third wave in educational uses of information technology', *CALICO Journal* 18(2), pp. 283–94

Noss, R. and Pachler, N. (1999). 'The challenge of new technologies: doing old things in a new way, or doing new things?', in Mortimore, P., *Understanding Pedagogy and its Impact on Learning*, pp. 195–211. London: Paul Chapman Publishing

Ofsted (2004a). *ICT in Schools – The Impact of Government Initiatives: Secondary English*. Retrieved on 15 August 2006 from http://www.ofsted.gov.uk/publications/index.cfm?fuseaction = pubs.summary&id = 3648

Ofsted (2004b). *ICT in Schools: The Impact of Government Initiatives Five Years On*. London: Ofsted

Pachler, N. (2001). 'Connecting schools and pupils: to what end?', in Leask, M., *Issues in Teaching Using ICT*, pp. 15–30. London: RoutledgeFalmer

Pisapia, J. (1994). *Teaching with Technology: Roles and Styles*. Metropolitan Educational Research Consortium, Virginia Commonwealth University, USA. Retrieved on 5 November 2006 from http://www.soe.vcu.edu/merc/briefs/brief5.htm

Ruthven, K., Hennessy, S. and Deaney, R. (2005). 'Incorporating Internet resources into classroom practice: pedagogical perspectives and strategies of secondary-school subject teachers', *Computers & Education* 44(1), pp. 1–34

Valentine, G., Marsh, J. and Pattie, C. (2005). *Children and Young People's Home Use of ICT for Educational Purposes: The Impact on Attainment at Key Stages 1–4*, Research Report 672. Nottingham: DfES

Conclusion

11 | Looking to the future, learning from success

This book has focused on two very different initiatives: the Iliad Project explored the place of oral literature in the primary curriculum and the Cambridge Online Latin Project (COLP) examined the contribution of ICT to the teaching and learning of Latin in secondary schools. But underlying the two projects is the same message about the need to make classics relevant and accessible. The continued presence of classics in schools depends on classicists being able to offer courses that not only present intrinsically interesting aspects of the classical world in an accessible format but also are in tune with the wider educational agenda. In the case of *War with Troy*, although it is the story itself that engages and motivates the pupils, from the teachers' point of view it is very important that the story provides opportunities to address pupils' literacy skills; and they very much appreciate the fact that the story is presented as a spoken not a written text because it makes the story accessible to the full ability range and enables the development of pupils' speaking and listening skills, aural comprehension in particular.[1] In the case of the Cambridge Online Latin Project, the focus on information and communication technology (ICT), with the creation of an extensive bank of digital resources and the development of online learning courses, has helped sustain interest in schools where Latin is already taught and has given pupils access to the subject for the first time in schools where it has never been offered.

For the foreseeable future at least, the place of classics in primary schools is secure because it is part of National Curriculum history. At secondary level, on the other hand, its position is very precarious. However, as others have noted (e.g. Gibbs 2003: 36), since 2000 the National Curriculum has gradually become less prescriptive and this

---

[1] The primary Latin course, *Minimus*, has been successful for similar reasons: in its case the emphasis is more on the formal grammatical elements of the National Literacy Strategy.

has eased the pressure on non-National Curriculum subjects. At the same time government initiatives such as the Gifted and Talented programme, together with the aggressive promotion of specialist schools, have signalled a desire to move away from a model of secondary education based on uniform provision of a minimum entitlement towards a more diverse model with greater emphasis on choice and opportunity for the individual. As a result many headteachers are more sympathetic towards classical subjects than at any time in the last twenty years, and classicists must be ready to exploit the slightest hint of an opening in the curriculum.

To examine what conditions need to be in place in order for classics to thrive in the modern curriculum, in the summer term of 2006 I interviewed the headteacher and the head of classics in three comprehensive schools with thriving classics departments, two in rural communities and one in outer London. Two of the three schools had introduced classics onto the timetable *since* the introduction of the National Curriculum; and all three schools offered both classical civilisation and Latin (and in one of the schools classical Greek was also available, and thriving, as a lunchtime club). In one school there was a one-person department supported by a member of the English department who shared the classical civilisation teaching; in another there were two full-time classics teachers who covered the whole of the classics provision themselves; and in the third the two classicists were supported by three teachers from other departments.

In many ways the interviews reinforced the lessons drawn from the Iliad Project and COLP. Both headteachers and heads of department stressed the importance they attached to classics being seen as an inclusive subject, catering for the full ability range; as a relevant subject, with clear links to the National Curriculum; and as an interesting and exciting subject, with ICT an integral part of most lessons. But the most important factors in the success of classics were:

- a strong commitment to classics from the headteacher;
- high-quality classroom teaching;
- the integration of the classics department in the school community.

Classics survives and flourishes in these schools because of the active support of the headteacher, but that support has been earned, and sustained, by the classics teachers and the quality of their classroom teaching. All three headteachers spoke with genuine warmth and conviction about the contribution made by classics to the school curriculum. At the same time all three were well aware of the part they themselves played in keeping the subject alive. One headteacher, an English and philosophy graduate, who had himself introduced classics into the school, was particularly forceful in his defence of the subject. In a recent curriculum review he had made it clear to staff from the outset that classics was a non-negotiable element of the Key Stage 3 curriculum. But he felt in a position to do so only because he could point to the fact that classics was offered to all pupils in Year 8 and was meeting children's wider educational needs by addressing aspects of literacy and citizenship. And the fact that the classics department was seen to be teaching the full ability range – rather than, say, just the top set in each year – strengthened its standing with colleagues in the staffroom, some of whom, in the words of the headteacher, had been 'a bit sniffy' at first about the introduction of classics because they thought it marked the first step towards introducing school uniform!

Overcoming misconceptions about classics is an important first step in persuading staffroom doubters that classics has a right to be included in the curriculum; and if, as in two of the schools, the classics department is also seen to make a significant contribution to the teaching of citizenship, classics is all the more likely to gain acceptance with colleagues. There are other ways that the classicists in the three schools have won over colleagues and avoided the isolation that all too many classics teachers feel, for instance by taking an active part in courses other than classics, as in the case of one head of department who teaches leisure and tourism GCSE as well as Latin and Classical Civilisation; and by involvement in the pastoral curriculum and other aspects of school life such as staff development (another head of department is the school's professional tutor responsible for trainee teachers). At a more informal level, colleagues can be made aware of the work of the classics department through accompanying classics groups on museum and theatre visits and, of course, visits to classical sites (these take place regularly in all three schools and are seen as a vital recruitment tool).

Above all, the classicists need to emphasise how much they have in common with their colleagues rather than how much they differ from them. This is the way to ensure that classics 'is interwoven into the fabric of the school', as one headteacher put it, and thereby guaranteed a long-term future in the curriculum.

Reference

Gibbs, M. (2003). 'The place of classics in the curriculum of the future', in Morwood, J. (ed.), *The Teaching of Classics*. Cambridge: Cambridge University Press

Appendix 1

GCSE Latin entries
by school type

	Maintained			Post 16	Independent	Other	Total
	Comprehensive	Grammar	Secondary modern				
1988	4,616	3,715	19	143	7,460	70	16,023
1989	4,355	2,807	25	188	8,323	107	15,805
1990	3,792	2,627	11	188	7,774	117	14,509
1991	3,272	2,292	12	156	8,019	70	13,821
1992	2,934	2,008	7	199	8,127	133	13,408
1993	2,693	1,964	0	149	7,552	272	12,630
1994	2,600	2,031	0	159	7,973	81	12,844
1995	2,479	1,905	0	142	8,332	100	12,958
1996	2,606	1,985	1	142	7,845	80	12,659
1997	2,202	2,083	0	115	7,409	51	11,860
1998	1,996	1,772	0	137	6,966	37	10,908
1999	1,787	1,833	0	118	6,669	44	10,451
2000	1,840	1,915	0	133	6,642	31	10,561
2001	1,936	1,852	0	62	6,500	15	10,365
2002	1,754	1,834	0	76	6,431	32	10,127
2003	1,856	1,825	0	77	6,227	19	10,004
2004	1,670	1,719	7	72	6,360	15	9,843
2005	1,707	1,586	0	95	6,340	15	9,743

Source: the AQA statistical division, Guildford

Appendix 2

Transcript of *War with Troy* episode 4, 'First Blood'[1]

From the city walls of Troy, the people, ranged along the walls on turrets and towers, saw a darkening on the horizon. They rubbed their eyes. They looked again and now they could see a thousand flecks of mast, each one with its little coloured rag of sail. They rubbed their eyes. They looked again and now they could see ships, a thousand ships slicing through the waves, each ship crammed with warriors.

And the Trojans wasted no time then. There was a harnessing of horses to chariots. There was a sharpening of swords. There was a buckling of breastplates and belts and greaves. There was a seizing of helmets and shields. The great bronze Scaean gates were thrown open and, with a whirring of wheels and a creaking of chariots and a neighing of horses, a shouting of men, a thundering of hooves and feet, the Trojan army poured across the plain. And with a crash of bronze against bronze, the Trojans met the Greeks wading ashore, as two rivers in full spate, each one with a flotsam of uprooted trees, might crash into one another. So it was the Trojans met the Greeks.

And, if I could sing now, I would sing of the Trojans' secret weapon – a warrior, whose name was Cygnus, standing head and shoulders above all other men. Cygnus, a son of Poseidon, the god of the sea – white-skinned, white-tongued, white-lipped, white-haired Cygnus – as white as sea foam, as white as the seventh wave of the sea. I would sing of Cygnus, whose skin was charmed against the striking of sword, dagger, spear, arrow or battleaxe. Cutting down Greeks with every stroke of his sword, with every thrust of his spear, while the Greek swords buckled against his skin, and the Greeks' spears glanced from him as if glancing from stone. I would sing of tremendous Cygnus, leaving a wake of dead behind himself as he fought.

One ship had yet to yield her cargo. From his ship Achilles watched, his heart in turmoil. From his ship Achilles watched the savage Cygnus cutting a path through the Greek ranks, like a plough

---

[1] This excerpt is reproduced with permission of the Cambridge School Classics Project.

Appendix 2 Transcript of War with Troy *episode 4, 'First Blood'*   161

through moist earth.

Aboard his ship, tethered to the mast, the four wonderful white horses that had been the gifts of Poseidon. Now one of them, Beauty, lifted his long head and said, 'Son of Peleus, you know the fate that hovers over you. You know if you set foot on these shores, yours will be a short life. Not for you the stretching shadow, not for you the ripening grape, not for you the joy of children. You are matchless in the field of battle. No man could ever harm you. But a god could.'

As Achilles listened, his face began to tingle, and then he said, 'My dear horse, you speak so rarely and yet you waste your words. I choose death! I choose death so that my name will live for ever on the tongues of men and women!' And, with a cry, he drew his sword, he stabbed the air and he leapt from his ship.

The Trojans saw him like a dancer, leaping through the air, and they saw him land, striking the sand with his foot. And, where he landed, a spring burst out of the ground. And then, as though running through long grass, he ran across the battlefield until he was standing in front of Cygnus.

'Know it was Achilles who killed you!' And, with all the strength of his arm, he hurled his spear at Cygnus. But the spear struck Cygnus and it clattered down to the ground at his feet, as though it was a reed that had been thrown by a little boy. And Cygnus lifted his arms and he laughed. And he said, 'Throw another one, my little friend. I know who you are. You are Thetis' son. But I'm no more afraid of you than of a mosquito that I might smear across my arm. From head to foot I'm charmed against the striking of all weapons.'

And Achilles drew his bronze sword then and, leaping and dancing and slashing to the left and the right, he attacked Cygnus with terrible ferocity, until Cygnus' armour was hanging from his body like a shattered eggshell. But still Cygnus was unscratched. And, laughing, he lifted his own spear and he hurled it at Achilles. And he struck Achilles' shield with such force that the point of the spear penetrated the gold and nine layers of hardened ox hide. And Achilles staggered backwards with the strength of the stroke.

But then he caught his balance and, with an expression of terrible, inhuman ferocity, his lips curled back from his teeth, he leapt at Cygnus. He smashed his shield into Cygnus' face. He ground the boss of the shield to the left and the right until Cygnus' nose was smeared across his cheek and his teeth were shattered.

And, as Cygnus staggered backwards, Achilles knelt on his shoulders. 'If weapons won't harm you, what will armour do?' He tore the helmet from Cygnus' head. He wrapped the helmet straps around his neck, twisting and tugging and tightening the tourniquet until Cygnus' head was half-torn from his body and every last shudder of life was gone from him.

And Achilles leapt to his feet, splattered with blood, shrieking with laughter. And the Trojan army stood and they stared, appalled, mesmerised.

And then a strange thing. The twisted, broken neck of Cygnus began to stretch and to curve. And his face narrowed and his lips stretched and hardened and out of his skin white feathers [grew]. His father Poseidon had taken pity on him and had transformed him into a swan. And now he was lifting his feathered arms and the shattered eggshell armour was falling away from him. He was beating his wings against the air. He lifted himself high and high and high into the sky. And three times he circled round. And the only sound was the sighing and the sawing of his wings. And then he flew over the sea, over the masts of the ships and he was gone.

And Achilles ran towards the Trojans, with his Myrmidons behind him. Achilles ran towards the Trojans, screaming and screaming. And the Trojans' hearts turned to water and they fled. They ran and they ran through the great bronze Scaean gates. The gates were closed behind them. And, from that day onwards, to any Trojan warrior the name Achilles was like a cold shudder from the nape of the neck to the root of the spine.

And, as for the Greeks, they loosed a few lazy arrows after the retreating Trojans and then they set about dragging their ships high onto the white sand.

Appendix 3

National Curriculum terminology

The years of compulsory education are divided into four Key Stages as follows:

Key Stage	Year	Age of pupils at start of academic year
KS1	Y1	5
	Y2	6
KS2	Y3	7
	Y4	8
	Y5	9
	Y6	10
KS3	Y7	11
	Y8	12
	Y9	13
KS4	Y10	14
	Y11	15

Index